"There are four primary areas c
of them is finances, and that is
cial challenges and questions. I would recommend this book ...
married or single, male or female, young or older ... Tom has
some very practical advice because he uses biblical principles
as guides. Anyone would benefit from reading this book and applying those principles."

—Jack Hannah, retired pastor,
Westney Heights Baptist Church, Ajax, Ontario

"Tom Copland provides insight into understanding God's word
as it applies for budgeting, spending wisely, and waiting on the
Lord. Tom has counselled thousands of people and led hundreds
of seminars including many for In Touch Ministry supporters. I
highly recommend this devotional because it is totally based
on Scripture and will bring your spending habits in line with
Scripture."

—Art Brooker, chairman of the board,
In Touch Ministries of Canada

"There was a time in my life when I was consumed with money
and material wealth: the hunt for them, the desire for more, and
the ensuing debt. I wanted all the things I could afford, and wanted them now. Allowing these idols caused me to act unethically
and turn a blind eye to God in this area. God is merciful and
showed me this sin, in love, which I took seriously and Jesus
redeemed it. It is now baffling to me how little I had been taught
in church or seminary or through other Christians on this—easily
argued—single most highlighted topic in Scripture. I believe this
to be a cunning trick of the Deceiver. With Tom Copland's God-
given humility and wisdom in this area, I sit under his authority
which is entirely scripturally based and Spirit-led. A quote from

Tom that changed my life: 'If you were called into full time ministry TODAY, could you go?'"

—C. Golberg, BRE, M.Div.

"Through Tom's course Financial Management God's Way, I came to appreciate that God has a plan and purpose for how we manage the money he has entrusted to us. Tom's passion and commitment to teaching God's financial principles has helped countless Christians break the bonds of debt and experience the life-changing power of God's word. 'Do not conform any longer to the pattern of this world but be transformed by the renewing of your mind' (Romans 12:2) This book will renew your mind and transform your life!"

—Anthony Martino, MBA, CPA

"For more than 15 years I have watched Tom's financial seminars change lives ... including mine. Tom carefully unpacks biblical truth and applies it to real financial situations that most people find themselves in at one time or another. In his new book *Biblical Principles that Will Transform How You Manage Money*, Tom takes the same tested, proven, and true principles from the seminars and puts them in book form. Here Tom has distilled the Bible's true and often countercultural truth as it relates to finances and presented it in a practical, hopeful way. I commend this book to you. If this truth changes your life the way it changed mine, your efforts will be well rewarded!"

—Pastor Don Symons, senior pastor at Westney Heights Baptist Church, Ajax, Ontario, and former executive with a large multinational technology company

"Hi Tom, I took your financial management God's way course last fall. With God's direction and your advice, I have paid off my mortgage!"

—B. C., Ontario, Canada

"Hi Tom, I just wanted to let you know that I was listening to your message years ago when we were working together. You've changed my life. I sold my larger house and minimized my life-style and set new financial goals because of the time you spent talking with me and the CDs you gave me. I was listening and I've made saving a priority. Thank goodness!"

—B. P., South Carolina, USA

"To Tom and staff, we want to say thank you! We have been watching your zoom study on 'Financial Management God's Way.' We have both learned so much and we never dreamed the Bible had so much to say on finances. We are currently following a budget and actively paying down our debt. Thank you for this awesome study!"

—L. A., Saskatchewan, Canada

"Thank you, Tom, for your faithfulness in teaching God's word on finances. This has been very much appreciated and I'm sending a donation to your ministry today."

—L. M., Ontario, Canada

"Tom, I listen to you almost every day on your show on Faith FM radio. I have learned so much and you have been a Godsend to me. I was praying for God to help me with an understanding of his law with respect to finances, and God blessed me with the best teacher/mentor I could've asked for. Thank you, Tom, and God bless you."

—Ellyna, Ontario, Canada

"Hi Tom, I just wanted to tell you what a blessing you have been in my life. You've taught me to study Scripture, always ensuring that my thoughts are consistent with Scripture. Ever since taking 'Financial Management God's Way,' I've tried to make sure that I have some Scripture as backup before I take an opinion on any money matter. It is changed many relationships for the better. Thank you!"

—**L. S., Ontario, Canada**

"Recently, a group of pastors were discussing that their churches are falling behind in giving and having trouble meeting budgets. I was able to share that our church was in fact ahead in this year's budget and we enjoyed a sizable surplus. Upon reflection, I concluded that one of the reasons for the excellent response was because Tom has been teaching some classes on what God's word says about finances with an emphasis on debt reduction. Often, people fail to give because they are carrying a heavy debt load. Further, I'm finding that debt is placing a tremendous stress on marriages and affecting people's emotional and physical health. One of the men who was baptized in our church testified to the fact that it was [Tom's] financial teaching that enabled him to get his spiritual priorities straightened out."

—**Pastor J. H., Ontario, Canada**

"Hi Tom, there has been a spiritual shift in my finances since taking your class. I'm now thinking differently about money. I continue to track my expenses diligently and formulate a budget every two weeks. God is blessing, and I'm paying down my debt. Thank you for the positive, life-changing impact you've made!"

—**J. C., Ontario, Canada**

"My name is Dario, and my wife and myself attended your seminar several years ago. Your seminar has helped us incredibly with our finances. We bought our house and paid it off in 13 years. Thank you, again!"

—**Dario, Ontario, Canada [originally from the Philippines]**

"Dear Mr. Copland, I have benefited greatly from your teaching as it has helped me change my thought process on handling my finances, planning for the future, and estate planning. I record your messages on my PVR so that I can watch them from time to time. So, thank you, again."

—**L. C., Quebec, Canada**

"I have been debt-free for a few years. The joy of being debt-free is tremendous. The funds I saved enable me to go for a few missions trips and to support other missions. I still receive your financial moments, which are very helpful, and track my expenses using the Copland budgeting system. Thank you for your teaching, and I will continue to pray for you."

—**J. N., Ontario, Canada**

FINANCIAL MOMENTS

WITH TOM COPLAND
(Chartered Professional Accountant)

*Biblical Principles that Will
Transform How You Manage Money*

Financial Moments with Tom Copland
Copyright ©2021 Tom Copland

Published by Castle Quay Books
Burlington, Ontario, Canada and Jupiter, Florida, U.S.A.
416-573-3249 | info@castlequaybooks.com | www.castlequaybooks.com

Printed in Canada.

Edited by Marina Hofman Willard
Cover design and book interior by Burst Impressions

978-1-988928-53-1 Soft Cover
978-1-988928-54-8 E-book

Library and Archives Canada Cataloguing in Publication

Title: Financial moments with Tom Copland : biblical principles that will transform how you manage
  money / by Tom Copland.
Names: Copland, Tom, 1953- author.
Identifiers: Canadiana 20210290137 | ISBN 9781988928531 (softcover)
Subjects: LCSH: Finance, Personal—Biblical teaching. | LCSH: Finance, Personal—Religious aspects—
  Christianity.
Classification: LCC HG179 .C6585 2021 | DDC 332.024—dc23

BIOGRAPHY

Tom Copland is a servant of the Lord Jesus Christ and a chartered professional accountant; since 1982, he has been called to teach God's word on finances. Tom has had the privilege of helping thousands of people learn God's way of managing money. Through his counselling, he has seen many of these individuals become completely debt-free.

Tom is the author of the "Financial Moments," which are one-minute summaries of biblical financial principles. Tom has recorded 371 "Financial Moments" that are currently aired on 155 radio stations and seven television stations across Canada and parts of the northern United States. It is estimated that more than two million people hear at least one "Financial Moment" every week.

Tom is also the author of *Financial Management God's Way*, an in-depth biblical financial study whereby people can learn God's way of managing money. The study's topics include how to get out of debt, a worldly versus a biblical perspective on money, budgeting, obtaining godly counsel, giving generously, investing, financial deceptions, stewardship, and how money management impacts relationships in marriages and with God.

In addition, Tom has led numerous workshops and webinars, on topics such as God's financial wisdom for business, biblically based estate planning, financial wisdom for young people, managing money during difficult times, and how to discern God's will for managing money. Tom has produced many other resources, including the Copland budgeting system. These resources are available from his website, www.coplandfinancialministries.org. Most of these resources can be accessed for free.

Tom owns and operates his own public accounting firm in Markham, Ontario, Canada. He and his staff provide biblically based financial advice to their clients, in conjunction with accounting and tax services.

The firm's website is www.copland-ca.com.

To my Lord and Saviour Jesus Christ,
who has called me to teach his word on finances.

"For God's gifts and his call are irrevocable"
(Romans 11:29).

XII. MANAGING MONEY DURING DIFFICULT TIMES, INCLUDING A PANDEMIC 157

ACKNOWLEDGEMENTS

I'd like to thank Henry Enriquez, my tech support, who has been so faithful for over 24 years in helping with my ministry—performing all kinds of tasks that are too numerous to mention. I'd like to thank Art Brooker, the chairman of the board of In Touch Ministries of Canada, who came up with the concept of the "Financial Moments"; he put me in contact with the appropriate people in radio and television in order to expand this ministry.

In addition, I'd like to thank Pastor Don Symons and Pastor Jack Hannah, the two pastors of my church, who have both been a great support, both personally and for the ministry God has called me to. And further, I would like to thank my very good friend Cam Golberg, who has been a great support over the last several years and a superb small group leader of the series "Financial Management God's Way." Finally, I'd like to thank Ilana Reimer for her excellent editing and Castle Quay Books for recognizing my vision and agreeing to publish the book.

PLEASE READ THIS BEFORE YOU BEGIN

I would like to share my heart as to how God has called me to teach his word on finances. Since 1982, God has spoken to me clearly on many occasions as to what he created me to do. Psalm 139:13–16 states:

For you created my inmost being; you knit me together in my mother's womb. I praise you because I am fearfully and wonderfully made; your works are wonderful, I know that full well. My frame was not hidden from you when I was made in the secret place, when I was woven together in the depths of the earth. Your eyes saw my unformed body; all the days ordained for me were written in your book before one of them came to be.

In other words, when God created me in my mother's womb, he had a *very specific plan and purpose for my life*, and that was to teach his word on finances. So, it's no coincidence that I became a chartered professional accountant even before I came to know the Lord. But more importantly, after I accepted Jesus Christ as my Saviour and Lord on April 12, 1981, God made it clear that his calling for my life was to teach and advise people on how they should manage the money entrusted to them according to biblical principles. As Romans 11:29 says, "For God's gifts and his call are irrevocable."

My heart's desire is to serve the Lord faithfully with 100 per cent of my effort while I'm here on earth. That's why I ask people to introduce me as a "servant of the Lord Jesus Christ." I don't believe I have any special talents; I'm simply a servant of the Lord who has been created and specifically called to teach his word on finances.

The purpose of this book is to teach what God's word, the Bible, says about finances. With over 2,300 references to money and material things, there is incredible wisdom in God's word. But unfortunately, most people are unaware of this wisdom, and as a result, they unintentionally violate biblical financial principles and later suffer the consequences. However, once individuals and couples learn God's way of managing money and purposely implement biblical financial principles in managing their monthly cash flow, they will end up much better off financially in the long term. Further, they will experience less financial stress and very often less marital conflict caused by financial problems.

In this book, there are numerous financial moments, each of which is a brief summary of a biblical principle on finances. These financial moments are grouped by topic, so if there's a particular topic you're interested in, such as debt, investing, or estate planning, you can quickly identify that section and read those financial moments. Having said that, I recommend that you read the entire book at least twice. The first time, you will gain a broader understanding of God's word on finances. As you go through the second time (more slowly), you can ensure that you're implementing these biblical financial principles into how you manage money.

Further, this book can be used as a daily devotional. As you read, you can meditate on the Scripture passages I quote and ask for God's wisdom regarding your personal financial circumstances. My hope is that even after you've read it, you'll consider this book a resource you can go back to whenever financial questions arise. Regardless of whether you have significant debt, no debt, or a surplus, you can benefit from reading this book and learning more about God's financial wisdom. The principles in this book are intended to help you experience God's peace in the area of finances (see John 14:27). Sadly, very few people experience this peace.

If you have any questions as you go through this book, feel free to send us an email at info@Biblefinance.org. Either myself or one of my financial coaches will answer your questions. In addition, if you need financial coaching, please complete the Copland budgeting system, and then send us an email with the completed form and an explanation of the financial problems you are encountering. Outlining your financial facts on our budgeting system will enable us to give you better biblically based financial advice. The Copland budgeting system, along with a half-hour instructional video on how to use it, are available on our website, www.coplandfinancialministries.org at no charge. We also provide financial coaching on a ministry basis at no charge.

—Tom Copland

I.
PEACE AND ANXIETY

1. God Gives Peace Regarding Finances
Financial problems cause stress and anxiety, but God can provide his peace. Jesus said in John 14:27, "Peace I leave with you; my peace I give you. I do not give to you as the world gives. Do not let your hearts be troubled and do not be afraid." Prayer is the first step to obtaining God's peace. Philippians 4:4–7 says:

> Rejoice in the Lord always. I will say it again: Rejoice! Let your gentleness be evident to all. The Lord is near. Do not be anxious about anything, but in every situation, by prayer and petition, with thanksgiving, present your requests to God. And the peace of God, which transcends all understanding, will guard your hearts and your minds in Christ Jesus.

In other words, in prayer, draw close to the Lord, and God will give you his peace, which is beyond your understanding. This is not something we can figure out or earn. It is a gift granted by God. "Now may the Lord of peace Himself continually grant you peace in every circumstance" (2 Thessalonians 3:16, NASB).

2. Focusing on God Brings Peace
Are you worried about financial problems? If yes, then remember that God promised to meet your needs if you put him first. In Matthew 6:31–33, Jesus said:

> "Do not worry, saying, 'What shall we eat? or 'What shall we drink?' or 'What shall we wear?' For the pagans run after all these things, and your heavenly Father knows

that you need them. But seek first his kingdom and his righteousness, and all these things will be given to you as well."

You should invest sufficient time to addressing your financial problems, but don't overdo it and constantly worry about finances. Take a break and focus on God, not your financial problems. "You will keep him in perfect peace, whose mind is stayed on You" (Isaiah 26:3, NKJV).

In other words, God promised his "perfect peace" if you focus on him and trust him to provide the wisdom and money you need. It's also important to study God's word on finances. Often, Christians unknowingly violate biblical principles, resulting in financial problems.

3. God Will Carry Our Financial Burdens

Are you burdened and worried about finances? In Matthew 11:28–30 Jesus said, "Come to me, all you who are weary and burdened, and I will give you rest. Take my yoke upon you and learn from me, for I am gentle and humble in heart, and you will find rest for your souls. For my yoke is easy and my burden is light."

Jesus gently encourages us to come to him, ask for his help, and then yoke ourselves with him—that is, depend on God to carry the heavy part of the load.

In Isaiah 46:4, God promised he will sustain us, no matter how difficult the circumstances. "Even to your old age and gray hairs I am he who will sustain you. I have made you and I will carry you; I will sustain you and I will rescue you."

When we maintain a close personal relationship with the Lord, spending time in his word and in prayer, God gives us his wisdom and his peace, enabling us to rest in him. "Rest in the LORD and wait patiently for Him; do not get upset because of one who is successful in his way, because of the person who carries out wicked schemes" (Psalm 37:7, NASB).

4. Practical Steps to Reduce Financial Stress

Here are four practical steps to reduce your financial stress:

1. Track your expenses for two or three months to determine where your money is going.
2. Develop and implement a budget so that you spend less than you earn. This will ensure you have a monthly surplus.
3. Use that surplus to pay down your most expensive debt first. Usually, this means paying off credit card debt; then pay down your other debts.
4. Save some money for emergencies.

Proverbs 21:20 says, "The wise store up choice food and olive oil, but fools gulp theirs down." And most importantly, spend quality time with the Lord daily, asking God for his wisdom and direction in managing money. In Isaiah 48:17, God promised, "I am the LORD your God, who teaches you what is best for you, who directs you in the way you should go."

5. God Is in Control

Even if your financial pressures are overwhelming, remember, God is still in control. "The LORD has established His throne in the heavens, and His sovereignty rules over all" (Psalm 103:19, NASB).

After God miraculously provided all the materials and labour needed to build the temple, David acknowledged God's sovereignty and power in this prayer. "Everything in the heavens and earth is yours, O Lord, and this is your kingdom. We adore you as being in control of everything. Riches and honor come from you alone, and you are the ruler of all mankind" (1 Chronicles 29:11–12, TLB).

In addition to being in control of everything, God is aware of your financial problems. Psalm 121:5 says, "The LORD watches over you." And in Isaiah 41:10, God promised to take care of you. "So do not fear, for I am with you; do not be dismayed, for I am your God. I will strengthen you and help you; I will uphold you with my righteous right hand."

6. God Has a Purpose in Our Trials

Psalm 139 tells us that God is aware of every detail of our lives— and that includes our financial problems. Although God does not cause our financial problems, he allows them to occur.

God has a purpose for any trial his children encounter. Perhaps you have unknowingly violated one or more of his financial principles, in which case the purpose of the trial would be to teach you something. Or perhaps your financial problems are God's way of pruning you, with the objective of causing you to bear more spiritual fruit, as Jesus said in John 15:2.

Either way, God is still in control. In Isaiah 46:10–11 he says:

"I make known the end from the beginning, from ancient times, what is still to come. I say, 'My purpose will stand, and I will do all that I please.' From the east I summon a bird of prey; from a far-off land, a man to fulfill my purpose. What I have said, that I will bring about; what I have planned, that I will do."

Because God is sovereign, we need to trust him completely. We must depend solely on him for the direction and strength we need when dealing with all our financial problems.

7. God Teaches Us Through Financial Problems

Since God is in control, why does he allow Christians to experience financial problems? For Christians who violate biblical principles, financial trials are a means for God to teach us his way of managing money. But what about Christians who have followed God's principles and still have financial problems?

In John 15:1–2, Jesus explained that in the same way that a gardener prunes a vine, God prunes his children by way of trials so we will depend on him more and remain continuously connected to him. If we remain close to him, we will bear more spiritual fruit.

In John 15:5 Jesus said, "I am the vine; you are the branches. If you remain in me and I in you, you will bear much fruit; apart from me you can do nothing." Christ is clear that we must have a close personal relationship with him in order to bear fruit that will count for eternity. Though pruning is painful, the results will be eternally beneficial.

8. God Will Bring Good Out of Financial Problems

Regardless of how difficult our financial problems are, God can solve them—either quickly or slowly. As indicated in Psalm 103:19 and many other Scriptures, God is in control. He is the King of kings and Lord of lords.

God has a purpose for every trial in the believer's life; he will bring some good out of every hardship. As Romans 8:28 says, "And we know that in all things God works for the good of those who love him, who have been called according to his purpose." For example, we often experience more spiritual growth during trials. In these times, God draws us closer to him.

Because God is in control and he loves us, we know that we can trust him to allow only those financial trials that are within his will. God will provide the wisdom, direction, and strength we need to endure any financial trial. Psalm 46:1 says, "God is our refuge and strength, an ever-present help in trouble."

9. There Is Hope for Your Financial Mess

Regardless of how difficult your financial problems are, God, with his "incomparably great power" (Ephesians 1:19), is able to solve any financial mess. If you're in financial difficulty, I recommend the following three actions.

Prayerfully, ask God for his wisdom in deciding what you should do. James 1:5–6 says, "If any of you lacks wisdom, you should ask God, who gives generously to all without finding fault, and it will be given to you. But when you ask you must believe and not doubt."

Meditate on God's word. The Bible has over 2,300 references and 16 parables from Christ that deal with money. God's word contains incredible wisdom on finances, and its principles often contradict the world's wisdom.

Develop a budget, and follow it to ensure you are spending less than you earn and use the surplus to pay down debt and save for future needs. A budget is a tool that will help you plan your finances. "The plans of the diligent certainly lead to advantage, but everyone who is in a hurry certainly comes to poverty" (Proverbs 21:5, NASB).

10. Joe and Linda Experience God's Peace

Over several years, Joe and Linda unintentionally spent more than they earned and accumulated debt. On three occasions, they restructured their debt, believing this would solve their financial problems. It did not.

Joe and Linda were so stressed they were considering a divorce. However, for the first time, they studied God's word and learned they had been violating several biblical financial principles.

They decided to meditate on key verses to change their mindset regarding money to align with a godly mindset. They were following the principle of renewing their minds set out in Romans 12:2. Joshua 1:8 has a similar command: "Keep this Book of the Law always on your lips; meditate on it day and night, so that you may be careful to do everything written in it. Then you will be prosperous and successful."

They developed and implemented a budget to ensure that they were spending less than they earned and used the surplus to pay down debt. Joe and Linda prayed regularly and experienced "the peace of God, which transcends all understanding" (Philippians 4:7). Within three years, they had paid off their credit cards and line of credit. Joe and Linda praise God for the wisdom in his word and for his peace, which enabled them to endure these trials.

11. Geoff and Jill Acknowledge God's Purpose in Financial Trials

Geoff and Jill were devastated when the bank evicted them from their home. Geoff had been out of work for three months. They had missed the last three mortgage payments because they were in debt and had no savings.

Geoff and Jill could not understand why God was allowing this to happen. They desperately prayed and searched God's word for an answer. As they studied Scripture, they realized that they had not followed God's financial principles. They assumed too much debt and had become a servant to the lender, a danger

Proverbs 22:7 warns against. Foolishly, they had no savings for emergencies, as Proverbs 21:20 advises.

Geoff and Jill learned and implemented God's financial principles. Within three years, they were debt-free and had a significant down payment for a new home. The couple now understands that the Lord's purpose in these trials was to draw them into a closer relationship with him and to teach them his way of managing money. The result was significant spiritual growth.

12. Are You Under Financial Stress and Don't Know What to Do?

If you are under financial stress, here is some biblically based financial advice.

Remember you're not alone. God has said, "Never will I leave you; never will I forsake you" (Hebrews 13:5). Do not worry. Instead, spend time with the Lord, and allow God—through his Holy Spirit—to pray on your behalf. Romans 8:26–27 says:

> The Spirit helps us in our weakness. We do not know what we ought to pray for, but the Spirit himself intercedes for us through wordless groans. And he who searches our hearts knows the mind of the Spirit, because the Spirit intercedes for God's people in accordance with the will of God.

Read God's word on finances, and ask him to speak to you through Scripture and his Spirit. Hebrews 4:12 says, "For the word of God is alive and active. Sharper than any double-edged sword, it penetrates even to dividing soul and spirit, joints and marrow; it judges the thoughts and attitudes of the heart."

Depend upon God (John 15:5). Seek his wisdom (James 1:5) and his specific direction (Psalm 32:8) in making any future financial decisions. Be sure to have Jesus's mindset, saying, "Yet not my will, but yours be done" (Luke 22:42).

Ask God to comfort you. Paul said in 2 Corinthians 1:3–4, "Praise be to the God and Father of our Lord Jesus Christ, the Father of compassion and the God of all comfort, who comforts us in all our troubles, so that we can comfort those in any trouble with the comfort we ourselves receive from God."

If you do these things, then God will direct you in making the wisest financial decision. Psalm 25:12 says, "Who, then, are those who fear the LORD? He will instruct them in the ways they should choose."

13. God's Word Is Priceless

If you want God's peace when it comes to your finances, study what the Bible says on the topic. As 2 Timothy 3:16–17 says, "All Scripture is God-breathed and is useful for teaching, rebuking, correcting and training in righteousness, so that the servant of God may be thoroughly equipped for every good work."

Most Christians unknowingly violate God's financial principles because of their lack of knowledge of his word on finances. Regularly meditating on God's word gives greater knowledge and understanding of God's financial wisdom (Joshua 1:8). It changes the way you think about money and material things (Romans 12:2). Once you develop "the mind of Christ" (1 Corinthians 2:16), you will be able to manage money God's way.

In John 14:26–27, Jesus said, "The Advocate, the Holy Spirit, whom the Father will send in my name, will teach you all things and will remind you of everything I have said to you. Peace I leave with you; my peace I give you. I do not give to you as the world gives. Do not let your hearts be troubled and do not be afraid."

In summary, allow God's word and his Spirit to direct you in making financial decisions.

14. Why Am I Experiencing All These Financial Problems?

Consider what 1 Peter 1:7 says:

> For a little while you may have had to suffer grief in all kinds of trials. These have come so that the proven genuineness of your faith—of greater worth than gold, which perishes even though refined by fire—may result in praise, glory and honor when Jesus Christ is revealed.

Financial problems can be extremely difficult. But when you continue to trust the Lord despite the challenges, this proves your faith is genuine and is of greater worth than gold (or money and other material things).

Paul assured us in 2 Corinthians 4:17–18, "For our light and momentary troubles are achieving for us an eternal glory that far outweighs them all. So we fix our eyes not on what is seen, but on what is unseen, since what is seen is temporary, but what is unseen is eternal."

In other words, don't focus on temporary material things such as money. Rather, focus on the rewards God will bestow upon Christians for eternity when they continue to put their faith and trust in him, notwithstanding their severe financial difficulties.

15. Are You Hurting Emotionally Due to Financial Problems?

Do you feel broken-hearted or oppressed? If yes, then don't worry—Jesus has this wonderful promise for you! "The Spirit of the LORD is upon Me, because He has ... sent Me to heal the brokenhearted, to proclaim liberty to the captives and recovery of sight to the blind, to set at liberty those who are oppressed" (Luke 4:18, NKJV).

Jesus understands your emotional and financial pain, and he wants to set you free. Here is God's promise:

"Because he loves me," says the LORD, "I will rescue him; I will protect him, for he acknowledges my name. He will call on me, and I will answer him; I will be with him in trouble, I will deliver him and honor him. With long life I will satisfy him and show him my salvation." (Psalm 91:14–16)

No matter how serious your financial problems are, God is greater! For example, in 2 Kings 4:1–7, Elisha miraculously provided oil for a widow and her son so she could pay all her debts. Regardless of your problems, God is able to heal you, both emotionally and financially.

16. Are You Crushed Due to Financial Problems?

Have you lost your job or your home, or are you drowning in debt? Remember, God is with you and has promised to help you. Psalm 34:18 says, "The LORD is close to the brokenhearted and saves those who are crushed in spirit."

Over the past 44 years, I've counselled thousands of people who were in so much debt their situations looked impossible. However, once they learned to manage money God's way, the Lord provided little miracles, such as unexpected income, a great deal on a purchase, or a gift from a fellow believer. In this way, the Lord enabled them to pay down their debts.

As David said in Psalm 23:1, "The LORD is my shepherd, I lack nothing." Later, in verses 5 and 6, he says, "You prepare a table before me in the presence of my enemies. You anoint my head with oil; my cup overflows. Surely your goodness and love will follow me all the days of my life, and I will dwell in the house of the LORD forever."

17. Are Your Financial Problems Causing You to Feel Depressed?

I encourage you to meditate on the following promises from God's word. Paul said in Romans 15:13, "May the God of hope fill you with all joy and peace as you trust in him, so that you may overflow with hope by the power of the Holy Spirit."

And remember that wonderful promise from God in Isaiah 40:31, "Those who hope in the LORD will renew their strength. They will soar on wings like eagles; they will run and not grow weary, they will walk and not be faint."

In other words, real hope comes only from God and his Holy Spirit as you trust him. The most practical way to experience God's hope and comfort during times of financial difficulty is to meditate on key Scriptures like the ones above. As the psalmist confirmed, "This is my comfort in my misery, that Your word has revived me" (Psalm 119:50, NASB).

Go to www.coplandfinancialministries.org to learn more about God's word on finances. We have numerous resources there, most of which are free. You can also follow @biblefinance on Facebook, Instagram, and Twitter.

II.
DEBT

1. God's Warning: Debt Is Dangerous

Many things entice us to borrow money. For example, you could receive offers of personal lines of credit or zero per cent financing or receive unsolicited credit cards. As a result many people believe these lies: "it's okay to buy now and pay later," or "smart people use other people's money."

These worldly beliefs are contrary to God's word. In Proverbs 22:7, God warned that "the borrower is slave to the lender." Why? Because if you are unable to pay your debts, there will be detrimental consequences.

Think about the following three examples.

1. Threats from creditors can generate tension between a husband and wife, often destroying their relationship.
2. A Christian is unable to accept a full-time job in ministry as the salary is insufficient to service their debts.
3. Debt causes stress, resulting in sleepless nights and health problems.

The absolute truth is that God wants us to be free to serve him and not a lender. God warns of the dangers of debt and strongly discourages borrowing.

2. Common Real-Life Case Study: Bob and Joan

Bob and Joan totalled their debts. They had several credit cards maxed to the limit, a personal line of credit, two car loans, and a large mortgage; in total, they had accumulated a huge amount of debt! How did this ever happen?

Reviewing their bank and credit card statements revealed that their spending had exceeded their income for many years. The couple realized borrowing money severely restricted their future options. To service their debts, Joan had to work full-time instead of staying at home with the kids, and Bob had to work additional hours.

As they studied what the Bible said about finances for the first time, the couple learned that God promised his children that if we put him first, he will meet our needs. In Philippians 4:19, Paul said, "My God will meet all your needs according to the riches of his glory in Christ Jesus."

Throughout the Bible, God consistently met needs without the assistance of a lender. Clearly, God wants his children to have little or no debt, so Bob and Joan committed to paying off all their debts as soon as possible.

3. Borrowing Presumes on the Future

When you borrow money, you are *presuming* you will have sufficient income in the future to service the debt. Since no one knows the future, there is a risk you will be unable to make the loan payments and experience financial difficulties.

In James 4:13–15, God warned:

Now listen, you who say, "Today or tomorrow we will go to this or that city, spend a year there, carry on business and make money." Why, you do not even know what will happen tomorrow. What is your life? You are a mist that appears for a little while and then vanishes. Instead, you ought to say, "*If it is the Lord's will, we will live and do this or that.*" (emphasis added)

Since only God knows the future, it is critical that you spend quality time with the Lord in prayer, to determine if it is God's will before you to borrow money. In Psalm 32:8, God promised, "I will instruct you and teach you in the way you should go; I will counsel you with my loving eye on you."

4. Questions to Consider Before Borrowing

I recommend that you consider the following four questions before borrowing money.

1. Have you prayed and given God a chance to provide the cash? We are told to "rest in the LORD, and wait patiently for him" (Psalm 37:7, KJV). In Deuteronomy 28, God promised his people that if they fully obeyed him, they would not have to borrow.
2. Is the item you plan to purchase a necessity? In Matthew 6, God promised that if we put him first, he will meet our needs, but not necessarily our wants and desires.
3. Have you prayed sincerely for God's direction? And if so, do you (and your spouse, if you're married) have peace that he wants you to borrow the money? Jesus said, "Peace I leave with you; my peace I give you. I do not give to you as the world gives" (John 14:27).
4. And finally, have you developed a budget beforehand to ensure you can afford the loan payments?

I encourage you to prayerfully ask these types of questions *before* you make any significant purchase.

5. Avoiding the Temptation to Borrow and Buy

Easy access to credit cards, personal lines of credit, and retailer incentives tempt us to borrow and buy.

One solution is to claim God's promise in 1 Corinthians 10:13, "No temptation has overtaken you except what is common to mankind. And God is faithful; he will not let you be tempted beyond what you can bear. But when you are tempted, he will also provide a way out so that you can endure it."

In other words, identify the types of spending temptations you struggle with, and avoid those temptations.

For example:

1. If you have a track record of overspending with credit cards, perform "plastic surgery" by cutting them up.
2. If you habitually spend too much at the shopping mall, then don't go there unless it's absolutely necessary. When you do have to go, bring a list and focus on what you need to purchase. Don't do any window shopping!
3. If you are a "tool guy," then purposely avoid the hardware store.

God is in control and has promised to meet our needs in Matthew 6:31–33. So we must be content to live within the income he has provided to us and avoid the many temptations to borrow and buy unnecessarily.

6. Recommendations for Avoiding the Temptation to Borrow Money

Here are some recommendations to avoid the many temptations to borrow money.

1. In prayer, ask God to enable you to learn to be content with his provision (Philippians 4:11–13).
2. Allow God to change the way you think about money and material things by renewing your mind. Romans 12:2 states, "Do not conform to the pattern of this

world, but be transformed by the renewing of your mind." How do you renew your mind? The answer is found in Joshua 1:8. "Keep this Book of the Law always on your lips; meditate on it day and night, so that you may be careful to do everything written in it. Then you will be prosperous and successful."

3. Study God's word on finances daily.
4. Before borrowing any money, prayerfully seek God's wisdom (James 1:5) and direction (Psalm 32:8) to determine if it's God's will.

I encourage you to implement these ideas and trust God (Proverbs 3:5–6) to enable you to avoid the many temptations of borrowing money.

7. Put God First and Trust Him to Meet Your Needs

Perhaps God's greatest financial promise to believers is that he will meet our needs, as we put him first. In Matthew 6:31–33, Jesus said:

> "Do not worry, saying, 'What shall we eat?' or 'What shall we drink?' or 'What shall we wear?' For the pagans run after all these things, and your heavenly Father knows that you need them. But seek first his kingdom and his righteousness, and all these things will be given to you as well."

Note that God has promised to meet needs such as food, clothing, and shelter, but he has not necessarily promised to meet our wants and desires. Often, what we believe to be needs in our life are really just things we want.

God has promised to meet our needs, and he doesn't need a bank, credit cards, or a personal line of credit in order to do so. In

Philippians 4:19, Paul said, "My God will meet all your needs according to the riches of his glory in Christ Jesus."

In summary, put God first and trust him, not a lender, to meet your needs.

8. God Meets Needs Through Little Miracles

Since 1982, I have counselled thousands of people who had a lot of debt—generally more debt than what they could personally pay back. However, when they started to manage their money God's way, God would provide "little miracles" of provision.

Sometimes, it was unexpected income, a great deal on a purchase, a better job, or a gift from a fellow believer. There are many examples of God's miraculous provision in the Bible. For instance, the Lord provided the Israelites with manna to eat for 40 years in the desert (Exodus 16); he gave a widow an abundance of oil so she could pay off her debts (2 Kings 4:1–7); and Jesus fed four thousand families with just seven loaves of bread and a few fish (Mark 8:1–9).

In summary, God does not need a lender to accomplish his will. He is the King of kings and the Lord of lords. Unfortunately, Christians often borrow money without asking God or waiting for his provision. In Matthew 6, God instructed us not to worry but rather to put him first, and he will meet our needs.

9. God Meets Needs Without Debt

Throughout the Bible, God met needs without creating debt. For example, in Deuteronomy, God promised his people that if they fully obeyed him, he would bless them, and they would be lenders, not borrowers:

If you fully obey the LORD your God and carefully follow all his commands I give you today, the LORD your God will set you high above all the nations on earth. All these blessings will come on you and accompany you if you obey the LORD your God ...

The LORD will send a blessing on your barns and on everything you put your hand to ...

The LORD will open the heavens, the storehouse of his bounty, to send rain on your land in season and to bless all the work of your hands. You will lend to many nations but will borrow from none. (Deuteronomy 28:1–13)

In 1 Kings 17, God used ravens to feed Elijah and miraculously provided flour and oil to the widow and her son during the famine. God's pattern throughout Scripture is to meet needs with no debt. However, the mindset of this world is to borrow money freely.

We shouldn't be surprised by this because, in Isaiah 55:8–9, God said: "'For my thoughts are not your thoughts, neither are your ways my ways,' declares the LORD. 'As the heavens are higher than the earth, so are my ways higher than your ways and my thoughts than your thoughts.'"

So before you borrow money, pray and ask God to meet your needs without debt. God is able!

10. God Blesses Obedience

Do you regularly study God's word on finances? Do you habitually seek the Lord's wisdom in managing your money? Unfortunately, many Christians inadvertently violate God's financial principles and accumulate debt. Worldly attitudes such as selfishness, covetousness, or lack of contentment cause them to spend more than they earn.

Most people live paycheque-to-paycheque with no budget; they make financial decisions based on personal desires or gut feelings without consulting the Lord. Deuteronomy 28 warns that debt is one of the results of disobeying God's financial principles. Here's what it says:

> However, if you do not obey the LORD your God and do not carefully follow all his commands and decrees I am giving you today, all these curses will come on you and overtake you …
>
> The foreigners who reside among you will rise above you higher and higher, but you will sink lower and lower. They will lend to you, but you will not lend to them. (Deuteronomy 28:15–44)

In summary, God will bless our obedience when we manage money his way. With over 2,300 references in the Bible to money, there is a lot to learn.

11. Contentment Results in Minimal Debt

One of the most biblical and practical ways to avoid borrowing money is to learn to be content with the income that God has provided. Why should we learn to be content? Because, as Paul said in 1 Timothy 6:6–8, "Godliness with contentment is great gain. For we brought nothing into the world, and we can take nothing out of it. But if we have food and clothing, we will be content with that."

How do we learn to be content? In Philippians 4:11–13, Paul explained:

> For I have learned to be content whatever the circumstances. I know what it is to be in need, and I know what it is to have plenty. I have learned the secret of being con-

tent in any and every situation, whether well fed or hungry, whether living in plenty or in want. I can do all this through him who gives me strength.

In summary, the secret to learning contentment is to focus on your relationship with Christ. In doing so, things that are of eternal value will become of greater importance to you than temporal things. Thus, this will significantly reduce your tendency to borrow and buy.

12. Have Hope: Don't Give Up on Your Financial Mess

Stressed out by financial problems? In Isaiah 41:10, God said, "Do not fear, for I am with you; do not be dismayed, for I am your God. I will strengthen you and help you; I will uphold you with my righteous right hand."

Here are four practical biblical steps to consider.

1. In prayer, ask God for his wisdom. As James 1:5 says, "If any of you lacks wisdom, you should ask God, who gives generously to all without finding fault, and it will be given to you."
2. Study God's word on finances. In Joshua 1:8, God said, "Keep this Book of the Law always on your lips; meditate on it day and night, so that you may be careful to do everything written in it. Then you will be prosperous and successful."
3. Develop and implement a budget to ensure you spend less than you earn and that you use the surplus to pay down debt.
4. Don't give up! Even if finances aren't your area of expertise, Jesus said, "My grace is sufficient for you, for my power is made perfect in weakness" (2 Corinthians 12:9).

In summary, even if you're in a financial mess, learn and apply biblical financial principles. God will meet your needs and enable you to pay down your debts.

13. Debt Restructuring Will Not Solve Your Financial Problems

Bill had no budget, lived paycheque-to-paycheque, and unintentionally spent more than he earned by accumulating debt on his credit cards. Once the credit cards were used to their limit, Bill paid them off with a personal line of credit. Three years later, Bill maxed out both his line of credit and credit cards.

In order to pay off these debts, he increased the mortgage on his house. Bill continued with his bad financial habit of spending more than he earned. Eventually, he had to withdraw money from his retirement account. Like most people, Bill believed that debt restructuring would solve his financial problems. This is not true.

Debt restructuring treats the symptom, not the problem. The problem was that Bill regularly spent more than he earned. Bill needs to learn and apply God's financial principles; he needs to develop and implement a budget to ensure he spends less than he earns and use the surplus to pay down debt.

14. Some Spiritual Problems Lead to Financial Problems

Many Christians believe their spirituality has no impact on how they manage money. This is not true. Sometimes, the root cause of financial problems is spiritual in nature. For example, the worldly mindsets of covetousness, lack of contentment, greed, selfishness, and pride will cause a Christian to manage money in a worldly fashion.

What's the solution? We must learn to think differently about money and material things. In Romans 12:2, God admonished us: "Do not conform any longer to the pattern of this world, but be transformed by the renewing of your mind."

How do we renew our minds? Joshua 1:8 says: "Keep this Book of the Law always on your lips; meditate on it day and night, so that you may be careful to do everything written in it. Then you will be prosperous and successful."

In summary, you should regularly study and meditate on God's word on finances to ensure you have a godly mindset with respect to money and material things.

15. Jim and Jennifer Learn God's Way of Managing Money

For the first time since they were married, Jim and Jennifer listed all of their debts. They were astonished when they realized how much money they owed: twenty thousand dollars of credit card debt, a forty-thousand-dollar personal line of credit, and a large mortgage!

Due to their financial problems, they were both stressed to the limit. But the good news was, Jim and Jennifer decided to study what the Bible had to say about finances. Much to their surprise, they had been violating many biblical financial principles for many years. For example, they had been living paycheque-to-paycheque with no budget, and they were unintentionally spending more than they earned.

With God's help, Jim and Jennifer learned to be content with a lesser lifestyle. They developed and implemented a budget to ensure that they were spending less than they earned. As a result, over the next three years, they were able to pay off their line of credit and credit cards. Wow! What a relief!

They now have a plan to pay off their mortgage within ten years. Jim and Jennifer praise God for his wisdom in his word. They wish they had understood and followed God's financial principles much sooner.

16. How to Get Out of Debt

Here are seven practical steps to get out of debt.

1. Pray and ask God to teach you and direct you. Isaiah 48:17 says, "I am the LORD your God, who teaches you what is best for you, who directs you in the way you should go."
2. Regularly study God's word on finances (1 Timothy 3:16–17).
3. Evaluate your present financial position. Most people make financial decisions based upon personal desires or gut feelings rather than their financial facts (Proverbs 27:23).
4. Develop and implement a budget to ensure you spend less than you earn, and use the surplus to pay down debt.
5. Ask God to enable you to be content with his provision (Philippians 4:11–13).
6. With your surplus of cash, pay down the most expensive debt first—usually, this means paying down your credit cards.
7. Depend upon God, follow up, and persevere until you are debt-free.

17. It Is Not a Sin to Borrow, but It Is a Sin to Borrow and Not Repay

Notwithstanding the Bible's warnings regarding debt, it is not a sin to borrow money. However, as indicated in Psalm 37:21, it is a sin to borrow and not repay it. In addition, it is a bad testimony when a Christian does not pay their debts. Jesus said, "Let your light shine before others, that they may see your good deeds and glorify your Father in heaven" (Matthew 5:16).

What kind of a "light into a world of darkness" is a Christian who doesn't pay their debts on time? Bankruptcy is not a biblical option for a Christian. It is a bad testimony and contrary to God's word.

Since 1982, I've counselled hundreds of Christians who were on the verge of bankruptcy. However, for those who learned and implemented God's financial principles, he enabled them to avoid bankruptcy and eventually pay their debts.

In summary, it is God's will that all Christians pay all of their debts on time.

18. A Biblical Approach Compared to a Worldly Approach

In this common real-life case study, "Mr. Unwise" manages money according to worldly financial principles, while "Mr. Wise" manages money according to biblical principles. Here's the comparison:

"Mr. Unwise" generally never saves; he just borrows and buys. He makes purchases based upon personal desires, not needs. He finances the purchase of a new car every three to four years. He buys a home with little down payment and has no budget. He runs a balance on his credit cards and experiences stress in the area of finances.

"Mr. Wise" spends less than what he earns and saves for future needs. He makes purchases based needs, not wants and desires. He drives a used car that doesn't incur debt. He saved a significant down payment for a home and pays it off as soon as possible. He lives within a budget, pays all of his debts on time, and experiences God's peace in the area of finances.

Are you more like "Mr. Unwise" or "Mr. Wise"?

Obtain my workshop series titled "Debt Reduction—God's Way," which is available at www.coplandfinancialministries.org for further help.

19. The Dangers of Christmas Debt

During Christmastime people often spend more than they can afford and accumulate debt. Credit cards, personal lines of credit, and overdraft privileges all entice us to get into debt.

The Bible provides examples of people with too much debt becoming a servant to the lender (2 Kings 4:1). The world's mindset is to buy now and pay later, but throughout Scripture, God met needs without creating debt. For example, consider the story of God working through Elijah to provide the widow and her son with flour and oil so they would not starve (1 Kings 17:9–16).

In Philippians 4:19, Paul said, "My God will meet all your needs according to the riches of his glory in Christ Jesus." In Matthew 6:31–33, Jesus promised that if you put him first, he will meet your needs, but not necessarily your wants and desires.

In summary, be very careful what you purchase this Christmas. Focus on needs, and avoid debt. If you use a credit card, make sure you have the funds to pay the statement in full when it's received. Remember, the true celebration is the birth of the Lord Jesus Christ, not the accumulation of material things.

20. Avoiding Future Christmas Debt

In the parable of the tower (Luke 14:28–30), Christ admonished us to plan ahead, which means we need to save for future needs. To accomplish this, we need to follow a budget to ensure that we spend less than we earn and have sufficient savings for future expenses. This would include Christmas gifts, annual insurance premiums, vacations, etc.

For example, if Christmas gifts cost about nine hundred dollars, you should save seventy-five dollars per month throughout the year so that you have sufficient funds and thus avoid debt. Saving is biblical. "The wise man saves for the future, but the foolish man spends whatever he gets" (Proverbs 21:20, TLB). How much do you need to save?

I recommend that you complete form three of the Copland budgeting system. It will enable you to calculate the required monthly savings to meet future expenses. The form is available as a free download at www.coplandfinancialministries.org. Also, be sure to watch the half-hour video that explains how to use the Copland budgeting system.

21. Summary of What God's Word Says on Debt

Here's a brief summary of what the Bible says on debt.

1. It is not a sin to borrow, but it is a sin to borrow and not repay (Psalm 37:21).
2. God discouraged debt and warned of its dangers (Proverbs 22:7).
3. The pattern throughout Scripture is for God to provide for our needs without us accumulating debt (Deuteronomy 28:01–12).
4. God has promised to meet our needs as we put him first; God does not need a bank to accomplish his promise (Matthew 6:31–33).
5. Debt restructuring will not solve your financial problems—it only treats the symptom (Proverbs 22:3).
6. We must learn to be content with God's provision (Philippians 4:11–13).
7. Contentment substantially reduces the tendency to borrow and buy (1 Timothy 6:6–8).

Before borrowing money, you should prayerfully ask the following questions:

1. Is this purchase a necessity?
2. Have I prayed and given God a chance to provide the cash or an alternative?
3. Have I developed a budget to ensure I can afford the loan payments?
4. Do I have God's peace before proceeding?

In summary, the world's mindset is to borrow and buy, but God's wisdom is to save for future needs.

Go to www.coplandfinancialministries.org to learn more about God's word on finances. We have numerous resources there, most of which are free. You can also follow @biblefinance on Facebook, Instagram, and Twitter.

III.
STEWARDSHIP

1. We Are Stewards of God's Money

What do the following verses say about owning money and material things?

Psalm 24:1 says, "The earth is the LORD's, and everything in it." In Job 41:11, God said, "Everything under heaven belongs to me." And David praised God with these words:

> "*Everything in the heavens and earth is yours*, O Lord, and this is your kingdom. We adore you as being in control of everything. Riches and honor come from you alone, and you are the ruler of all mankind; your hand controls power and might, and it is at your discretion that men are made great and given strength." (1 Chronicles 29:11–12, TLB; emphasis added)

What do these verses say about the ownership of money and material things? Since the absolute truth is that God owns everything, then logically, we are stewards or managers of the money and material things he has entrusted to us. God is the owner. As stewards, we need to look to the owner (God) for how we should manage his resources.

With over 2,300 references in the Bible to money and material things, God has much instruction for us. In summary, acknowledge God's ownership, and learn and apply his financial principles so you can fulfill your stewardship responsibilities.

2. Biblical Stewardship

In Haggai 2:8, God said: "The silver is mine and the gold is mine." At the time these Scriptures were written, silver and gold were used as money. So God is saying all money is his. Therefore, we are stewards of the money God has entrusted to us, while God is the owner.

In Psalm 50:7–12, God reminds his people, "Listen, my people, and I will speak … I am God, your God … for every animal of the forest is mine, and the cattle on a thousand hills … *the world is mine, and all that is in it*" (emphasis added).

In other words, God owns absolutely everything on this earth. Therefore, we are stewards or managers of the money and material things he has entrusted to us for the relatively short time— compared to eternity—that we are on this earth. As God's stewards, we must utilize money and material things according to God's principles and specific will.

3. Our Stewardship Responsibilities

Christian stewardship means acknowledging—in heart and mind—that God owns everything, and using money and material things in accordance with God's principles and specific will.

To accomplish this, we should habitually spend quality time with the Lord in prayer, asking for his wisdom in managing the money God has entrusted to us. We should study and meditate on God's word with regard to finances (Joshua 1:8) in order to change the way we think (Romans 12:2) with respect to managing money.

Of interest, 16 of the parables Christ gave us provide instructions for dealing with money. As a matter of fact, Christ spoke more about money management than any other topic.

And of course, manage money according to God's specific will, and trust him to meet your needs and direct you. "Trust in the LORD with all your heart, and lean not on your own under-standing; in all your ways acknowledge Him, and He shall direct your paths" (Proverbs 3:5–6, NKJV).

4. God's Financial Promises

God requires that we fulfill our stewardship responsibilities. That is, we should acknowledge in our hearts and minds that he owns everything and manage our money according to God's principles and specific will.

If we fulfill our stewardship responsibilities, God promises to meet our needs (Philippians 4:19; Matthew 6:31–33). Through-out the Bible, God promised to meet our needs, but not neces-sarily to satisfy our wants and desires. Sometimes what we think are needs, are really just things we want.

Further, as we fulfill our stewardship responsibilities, God will direct us. Psalm 25:12 says, "Who, then, are those who fear the LORD? He will instruct them in the ways they should choose."

In summary, if we manage the money God has entrusted to us according to his principles and his will, then God will direct us and meet our needs.

5. All Material Wealth Comes from God

From Genesis 1, we know that God created everything on this earth. We have an account in 1 Chronicles 29 of how God miraculously worked through his people to provide the required materials and labour to build his temple.

Haggai 2:8, says, "The silver is mine and the gold is mine." And in Leviticus 25:23, God instructed his people, "The land must not be sold permanently, because the land is mine."

The Bible is clear that all material wealth comes from God, and therefore we need to use the money and material things he has entrusted to us according to his will, not our will. Jesus said, "Yet not my will, but yours be done" (Luke 22:42). You can determine God's will by learning his financial principles and prayerfully asking him for his specific direction. Isaiah 58:11 promises, "The LORD will guide you always."

6. God Gives Us the Ability to Earn Income

Deuteronomy 8:17–18 provides the following warning to those who are successful. "You may say to yourself, 'My power and the strength of my hands have produced this wealth for me.' But remember the LORD your God, for it is he who gives you the ability to produce wealth."

And 1 Corinthians 4:7 states, "For who makes you different from anyone else? What do you have that you did not receive? And if you did receive it, why do you boast as though you did not?" Ephesians 2:10 states, "For we are God's handiwork, created in Christ Jesus to do good works, which God prepared in advance for us to do."

In conclusion, as God's workmanship, we must acknowledge in our hearts and minds that God gave us all of our natural abilities, including the ability to earn a good income. Therefore, we must humbly thank God for his blessings. And as stewards, we must utilize our natural abilities and money in accordance with God's principles and will.

7. We Are Individually Accountable to God

In the parable of the talents in Matthew 25, the master (God) entrusted different amounts of money to three servants, each according to their ability. The servant with five talents gained five more; the servant with two talents gained two more; but the servant with one talent buried his, making no effort to invest his master's money.

In the parable, God commended the servant who had two talents and earned two more, just as the one who had five talents had earned five more. The master said, "Well done, good and faithful servant! You have been faithful with a few things; I will put you in charge of many things. Come and share your master's happiness!" (Matthew 25:23).

In conclusion, each one of us is individually accountable to God in managing the money that he has entrusted to us—regardless of how much other people have. Faithful stewardship will result in God's blessings and additional resources from the Lord.

8. God Punishes Poor Stewardship

In the parable of the talents, God rewards the two faithful servants who worked to double their master's money. However, God judged the unfaithful servant, who buried his one talent, making no effort to invest his master's money.

God said, "So take the talent from him and give it to him who has the ten talents. For to everyone who has will more be given, and he will have an abundance. But from the one who has not, even what he has will be taken away" (Matthew 25:28–29, ESV).

"Everyone who has" means that to everyone who has been a faithful steward—managing money God's way—God will entrust with more. However, "the one does not have" represents unfaithful stewards whom God will punish by taking away whatever they have been entrusted with.

Therefore, let's be faithful stewards of God's resources by acknowledging in our hearts and minds that God owns everything and then using money and material things in accordance with his principles and specific will.

9. God Requires Faithfulness

All of us are accountable to God as to how we manage money and material things, regardless of the amounts he has entrusted to us. In 1 Corinthians 4:2, we read, "Now it is required that those who have been given a trust must prove faithful."

Faithfulness to God is critically important. As demonstrated in the parable of the talents (Matthew 25), God gives different amounts of money and material wealth to different people. Often, people believe they are not accountable to God because they don't have a lot of money. This is not true. Romans 14:12 states, "So then, each of us will give an account of ourselves to God."

In summary, the key issue from God's perspective is not how much money you have, but rather, whether or not you have been faithful with the money and material things he has entrusted to you. I'd encourage you to prayerfully consider this question: Are you managing money God's way?

10. Faithful Stewardship Does Not Require Significant Income

Some Christians believe they need significant income to be good stewards. This is not true. In the story of the widow, wealthy people gave significant amounts while the poor widow put in two very small copper coins. Yet Jesus said, "This poor widow has put in more than all the others. All these people gave their gifts out of their wealth; but she out of her poverty put in all she had to live on" (Luke 21:2).

In other words, if your income is modest, you should never feel that your contributions to God are insignificant. The Lord looks at the heart (Proverbs 16:2) and assesses generous giving and biblical stewardship based upon what he has entrusted to you.

As for wealthy people, the Bible provides examples of godly men (such as Abraham, David, Solomon, and Job) to whom God entrusted significant wealth and yet who were still faithful stewards of God's resources.

In summary, demonstrate your faithfulness to God in managing his money according to biblical principles and God's specific will, regardless of your level of income.

Go to www.coplandfinancialministries.org to learn more about God's word on finances. We have numerous resources there, most of which are free. You can also follow @biblefinance on Facebook, Instagram, and Twitter.

IV.
MONEY AND YOUR RELATIONSHIP WITH YOUR SPOUSE

1. Money Management Impacts Your Relationship With Your Spouse

Most people believe how they manage money has no impact on their relationship with their spouse. This is not true. Almost every week, someone calls me (it could be the wife or the husband) indicating that they and their spouse are having financial difficulties. Generally, one or both spouses have been violating God's financial principles by spending more than they are earning and accumulating debts. This results in stressful arguments between husbands and wives, which can destroy the marriage relationship.

Without my asking anything about their relationship, frequently these couples will share that their marriage is in serious trouble. So often, what started out as an unresolved financial problem many years ago has developed into significant relationship problems. These problems can be serious. If they are not dealt with quickly, they will likely result in separation or divorce.

In summary, I recommend you and your spouse learn to manage money God's way; it will significantly increase the success of your marriage.

2. Do Not Ignore Financial Problems

About one third of the people we counsel at Copland Financial Ministries are separated or divorced. In almost every case, they indicate finances were the most common area they and their ex-spouse argued about. Of interest, in most of the cases, there was enough income to cover their needs. Unfortunately, either one or both spouses were violating God's financial principles— typically by buying things they really didn't need with money they didn't have and accumulating debts.

Debt causes stress and heated arguments between husbands and wives. My advice to couples is this: do not ignore your financial problems because long-term, these problems can easily destroy your marriage relationship. Proverbs 22:3 says, "The prudent see danger and take refuge, but the simple keep going and pay the penalty."

So if you and your spouse are having financial problems, do not just restructure the debt or ignore your financial problems. Instead, be prudent and learn God's way of managing money. It could very well save your marriage.

3. A Husband Spends Unnecessarily and Accumulates Debt

Men and women often have different areas of financial temptation. Here's a common example for the men.

A wife calls me explaining that she and her husband are in a financial mess. Recently, her husband purchased a new vehicle with zero per cent financing, and bought numerous tools he didn't need on credit—all without consulting her and without developing a budget to see if they could afford the loan payments.

As a result, the wife is very angry with her husband. She indicates that she has withdrawn from her husband emotionally and physically, and that the relationship has deteriorated further.

I encouraged her not to allow bitterness take hold of her heart, because as the Bible says, "Do not let the sun go down while you are still angry, and do not give the devil a foothold" (Ephesians 4:26–27). And to husbands, I warn you, if you buy things you don't need and accumulate debt, it can easily destroy your physical and emotional intimacy with your wife.

4. A Wife Spends Unnecessarily and Accumulates Debt

Men and women often have different areas of financial temptation. Here's a common example for the women.

A wife regularly goes to the shopping mall, buying things she does not need on a credit card. The accumulation of debt triggers arguments with her husband. Over time, the husband withdraws from his wife emotionally. Since her emotional needs are not met, she withdraws from him physically and the marriage relationship goes into a downward spiral.

Ladies, if you spend money unnecessarily and accumulate debt, it can destroy your relationship with your husband. For both wives and husbands, remember that God has promised to meet our needs, not necessarily our wants and desires (Matthew 6:31–33). The Lord wants us to learn to be content with his provision.

In 1 Timothy 6:6–8, Paul said, "Godliness with contentment is great gain. For we brought nothing into the world, and we can take nothing out of it. But if we have food and clothing, we will be content with that."

And husbands, I encourage you to not let bitterness take hold of your heart, because it can give the devil a foothold in your life (Ephesians 4:26–27).

5. Avoid Unnecessary Expenditures

When I provide financial counsel to couples who are in debt, I encourage them to review their credit card statements, bank statements, and other statements over the last couple of years and identify unnecessary purchases. The reason I ask couples to do this is because often, a significant portion of the accumulated debt was incurred on unnecessary expenditures. Because of the accumulated debt and the related stress, in due course, couples begin arguing about finances.

Remember that God has promised to meet our needs, but not necessarily our wants and desires. In Matthew 6:31–33, Jesus said:

> "Do not worry, saying, 'What shall we eat?' or 'What shall we drink?' or 'What shall we wear?' For the pagans run after all these things, and your heavenly Father knows that you need them. But seek first his kingdom and his right-eousness, and all these things will be given to you as well."

In summary, do not allow the availability of credit to tempt you to buy things you do not need and get into debt. Doing so can easily destroy your marriage relationship. Rather, prayerfully review God's financial principles, and discern God's specific will before you make any major financial decision.

6. Advice to Couples in Financial Trouble

Are you and your spouse stressed out about finances? Have you accumulated a lot of debt? If yes, here are four recommendations that will help you get your finances in order.

1. Study God's word on finances (2 Timothy 3:16–17) because most Christians unknowingly violate biblical financial principles and later suffer the consequences.
2. Develop and implement a spending plan or budget with your spouse to ensure you spend less than you earn so you have a surplus to pay down debt and save for future needs (Luke 14:28–30).
3. Obtain biblical financial counsel. Proverbs 15:22 says, "Plans fail for lack of counsel, but with many advisers they succeed."

4. Meditate on key Scriptures so that God through his word and his Spirit can change the way you think about money and material things (Romans 12:2; Joshua 1:8; and Hebrews 4:12–13).

As you and your spouse manage money God's way, the financial stress will be relieved and your marriage relationship can be healed!

7. Biblical Management of Money Restores Marriage

Several years ago, a pastor called me explaining that he had been counselling a couple whose marriage was in serious trouble. They had separated and he did not think the marriage could be saved. However, because they argued so often about finances, he referred them to me.

I connected with this couple and obtained an understanding of their financial problems. I taught them God's way of managing money and helped them develop and implement a budget. I also provided several key Scriptures for them to meditate on related to the financial temptations they were struggling with.

They went through my in-depth biblical financial study, "Financial Management God's Way." God, through his word and Spirit, enabled them to change the way they managed their money (Romans 12:2).

Several months later, the husband thanked me for the financial advice and explained that with the release of the financial pressures, their relationship had healed, and they fell in love again! Here's what is interesting: I only provided biblically based financial advice; I did not provide any marriage counselling.

If finance is an area you and your spouse commonly argue about, be sure to get some biblically based financial advice. Copland Financial Ministries has financial coaches who give biblically based financial advice at no charge. If you're interested, go to our website www.coplandfinancialministries.org, or send an email to info@biblefinance.org.

8. Dealing With Your Financial Temptations

Almost everyone has areas of financial temptation. In order to deal with these, in 1 Corinthians 10:13, Paul said, "No temptation has overtaken you except what is common to mankind. And God is faithful; he will not let you be tempted beyond what you can bear. But when you are tempted, he will also provide a way out so that you can endure it."

In other words, everyone needs to identify their area of financial temptation and avoid those temptations. For example, if you are interested in tools or cars, avoid the hardware store and don't check out the vehicles at the local dealership. If you tend to spend unnecessarily at the shopping mall, don't go there. Or if you really have to, bring a list, purchase only what you need, and don't do any window shopping. In Hebrews 13:5, Jesus said, "Be content with what you have."

9. Long-Term Implications of Mismanaging Money

Besides destroying marriages, there are some other long-term negative implications that can arise when someone spends more than they earn and accumulates debts.

For example, if you develop a bad credit rating, it will likely create major problems for you and your spouse when you go to renew your mortgage with the bank. The banker will do their normal credit check and, if you have a bad credit rating, the banker will likely turn you down. This will force you to go to a secondary lender and pay a higher interest rate, and perhaps a mortgage brokerage fee.

Even if you decide to rent a home, most landlords will check your credit rating. If your rating is bad, you may not even be able to rent a home. Further, some employers will not hire individuals with a bad credit rating, so you could miss some really good job opportunities.

All of these situations can cause significant stress on your marriage and your other relationships as well. In summary, there is no substitute for learning to manage money God's way. It will greatly help your finances and ensure the stability and happiness in your marriage.

10. Management of Money Impacts Your Children

How parents manage their money can have a very significant impact on how their children will manage money as adults. In my experience, if parents mismanage money by buying things that they don't need with credit and accumulating debts, then generally their children will follow the same pattern when they become adults.

And if their children mismanage money as adults, their grandchildren will likely follow the same pattern. This is no surprise because in Exodus 20:5, God indicates that the sins of parents can be easily passed to the third and fourth generation. However, if the parents manage money God's way, and if they teach their children God's financial principles, then it is highly probable their children and grandchildren will follow the same pattern!

Proverbs 22:6 says, "Start children off on the way they should go, and even when they are old they will not turn from it." So you need to learn and apply God's financial principles so you can demonstrate a biblical example for your kids. This involves teaching your children God's word on finances, including giving, saving, and learning to be content with God's provision. Biblical teaching will shape the way your children manage money—probably for the rest of their lives!

11. Meditate on God's Word

If you are like most people, you probably have some bad financial habits and worldly thinking about finances. This can result in an accumulation of debt and create stress in your marriage.

In order to change the way we think about money and material things, God instructs us to habitually review and meditate on his word.

> These commandments that I give you today are to be on your hearts. Impress them on your children. Talk about them when you sit at home and when you walk along the road, when you lie down and when you get up. Tie them as symbols on your hands and bind them on your foreheads. Write them on the doorframes of your houses and on your gates. (Deuteronomy 6:6–9)

In other words, meditate on God's word with respect to finances. Discuss it with others, and teach it to your children. God's word is powerful. Hebrews 4:12 states, "The word of God is living and active. Sharper than any double-edged sword, it penetrates even to dividing soul and spirit, joints and marrow; it judges the thoughts and attitudes of the heart."

For example, if you struggle with selfishness or lack of contentment, then meditate on Philippians 4:11–13, which says:

> I have learned to be content whatever the circumstances. I know what it is to be in need, and I know what it is to have plenty. I have learned the secret of being content in any and every situation, whether well fed or hungry, whether

living in plenty or in want. I can do all this through him who gives me strength.

12. It Should Be Our Money—Not His Money or Her Money

Some married couples keep their money separate. Generally, this is not God's will. The Lord wants husbands and wives to become "one flesh" (Genesis 2:24). This implies that couples need to see their earnings as "our money," not "his money" or "her money." As well as putting all of their earnings into a joint bank account, a husband and wife should develop and implement a spending plan/budget together and agree on lifestyle decisions.

The only exception to sharing finances and financial decisions is if one spouse is irresponsible with money—for example, if one spouse buys unnecessary things and accumulates significant debts to the point where critical bills such as mortgage payments are put at risk.

When this occurs, it may be necessary for the responsible spouse, who manages money God's way, to exercise some tough love. This spouse may need to take control of the finances by depositing paycheques into their own bank account to ensure that the bills are paid and that the family's needs are met.

13. Be Honest With Your Spouse About Money

Generally speaking, husbands and wives should be totally open and honest with each other regarding their finances. For example, each individual should track their expenses and make that information available to their spouse. God wants husbands and wives to work together in managing the money he has entrusted to them. Further, most people will spend less when they know their spouse is going to see where their money is going.

Over the years, I've seen many cases where one spouse has accumulated debt on a credit card that the other spouse was unaware of. Often when the couple goes to renew their mortgage, the banker will do a standard credit check, revealing the debt caused by the bad money manager.

When this happens, the responsible money manager feels cheated and betrayed. Trust is critical for a good married relationship. Hidden debts will almost always be revealed at some point and will destroy that trust between spouses. "Lies will get any man into trouble, but honesty is its own defense" (Proverbs 12:13, TLB).

I recommend that you be totally open and honest with your spouse about money.

14. Financial Advice to Engaged Couples

In my experience, most couples do not discuss finances in any depth before they get married. Most feel their love for each other will overcome any potential problems they may face. This is generally idealistic. Finances are the most common area that married couples argue about.

Before couples get married, I recommend they fully disclose their debts to each other. Debt surprises after the wedding day can cause tremendous relationship problems, as one spouse may feel deceived and cheated by the spouse who has brought a lot of debt into the marriage.

In addition, couples should have an open and honest conversation about lifestyle expectations (for example, where they will live and how many cars they will drive) and prepare a budget to determine if they will be able to afford these lifestyle expectations.

If their income doesn't match their plans, they will need to learn to be content with less and lower their lifestyle expectations, as Paul talked about in Philippians 4:11–13. In summary, discuss finances in detail before you get married.

To learn more, watch my 18-minute video titled "Biblical Advice for Engaged Couples," which is available on our website, www.coplandfinancialministries.org.

15. An Engaged Couple Learns God's Way of Managing Money

A young couple was planning to get married. Before the wedding day, she noticed he spent money rather freely on credit cards. She asked to see his credit card statements and was astonished at how much money he owed. She spoke to him about his mismanagement of money. He didn't see it as a problem and assured her that because of their love, everything would work out just fine.

She prayed and she did not have God's peace (John 14:27) about marrying the young man, so she called off the wedding. He was shocked and in tears. The good news was that not long after, he decided to learn God's way of managing money. He went through an in-depth biblical financial study, developed a budget, and started to pay down his debts. As a result, about one year later, she decided to marry him after all. Today, this couple is teaching other people God's way of managing money!

If you're interested in my in-depth biblical financial study titled "Financial Management God's Way," be sure to go to our website, www.coplandfinancialministries.org. You can purchase a copy of the book and/or watch the online interactive videos. Through this study, we've seen significant permanent change in the way people manage money.

16. Review Your Past Expenditures

Whenever a couple or an individual has accumulated significant debts, I generally encourage them to review their credit card statements and bank statements over the last couple of years and identify any unnecessary purchases. Often, a significant portion of the accumulated debt was unnecessary.

As indicated in Matthew 6:31–33, God promises to meet our needs but not necessarily our wants and desires. So, the unnecessary expenditures need to be eliminated, and you need to learn to be content with less (Philippians 4:11–13). Paul's secret to learning contentment was to focus on his relationship with Christ and things of eternal value. When you do that, material things become much less important and you will spend less.

In Colossians 3:1–2, Paul said, "Since, then, you have been raised with Christ, set your hearts on things above, where Christ is, seated at the right hand of God. Set your minds on things above, not on earthly things."

17. Summary Comments on Managing Money Within Marriage

Throughout this topic of "Money and Your Relationship With Your Spouse," I've taught God's word on finances. I have provided some practical warnings that if you or your spouse violates God's financial principles, the financial stress can very easily hurt or destroy your relationship.

Of interest, about one third of the people whom we counsel in our ministry are separated or divorced. In most cases, these couples had enough money, but unfortunately, either one or both spouses spent more than they earned and accumulated debts. This resulted in tension, eventually destroying these marriages.

This is unnecessary. Both husbands and wives should learn to manage money God's way, including following a budget, learning to be content with less, and developing godly thinking with respect to money and material things. If they do so, then not only can their financial pressures be relieved, but it can help restore their marriages and they can fall in love again!

To learn more about how money management impacts your relationship with your spouse, watch my half-hour video on the topic, located at www.coplandfinancialministries.org. We have numerous other resources available there, most of which are free. You can also follow @biblefinance on Facebook, Instagram, and Twitter.

V.
RELATIONSHIP WITH GOD

1. Determine God's Will Before You Act

Often, as Christians, we make financial decisions without consulting the Lord. Then we pray later, asking God to bless our decisions. When we make financial decisions on our own, we will usually miss out on God's blessings. Our mindset needs to be the same as Christ's, who said, "Not my will, but yours be done" (Luke 22:42).

For those who prayerfully seek God's will, God will provide his wisdom (James 1:5) and specific direction. Psalm 25:12 says, "Who, then, are those who fear the LORD? He will instruct them in the ways they should choose."

Why? Because God knows what is best for us, and he wants to direct us. Isaiah 48:17 says, "I am the LORD your God, who teaches you what is best for you, who directs you in the way you should go."

In summary, prayerfully sense God's will before you make any important financial decision.

2. Overcoming Our Sinful Nature

In trying to manage money God's way, often we encounter a spiritual struggle that Paul described in Galatians 5:16–18, "So I say, walk by the Spirit, and you will not gratify the desires of the flesh. For the flesh desires what is contrary to the Spirit, and the Spirit what is contrary to the flesh. They are in conflict with each other, so that you are not to do whatever you want."

For example, sometimes our sinful nature causes us to buy things we don't need and can't afford. You can overcome your sinful nature and experience God's peace in the area of finances when you allow God, through his Holy Spirit, to control your mind (and therefore your actions). Romans 8:6 says, "The mind governed by the Spirit is life and peace."

In summary, we can overcome our sinful nature by deliberately and prayerfully allowing God, through his Spirit, to control our minds. Then we will experience God's peace in the area of finances and learn to manage money the Lord's way.

3. Abide in Christ

The Bible provides financial guidelines within which we must operate. However, sometimes there are several options within those guidelines. To ensure you are managing money according to God's specific will, you need a close personal relationship with the Lord.

In John 15, Jesus calls this "abiding." He says, "Abide in Me, and I in you. As the branch cannot bear fruit of itself, unless it abides in the vine, neither can you, unless you abide in Me. I am the vine, you *are* the branches. He who abides in Me, and I in him, bears much fruit; *for without Me you can do nothing*" (John 15:4–5, NKJV; emphasis added).

In the same way that a branch cannot bear fruit unless it remains connected to the vine, we cannot bear fruit unless we remain in a close relationship with Christ. Therefore, I encourage you to develop and maintain a close personal relationship with the Lord so you can manage money according to God's principles and specific will.

4. Time With the Lord in Prayer

In order to manage money God's way, you need to spend quality time with the Lord each day in prayer, asking for his wisdom (James 1:5), and listening for his answers.

Jesus said, "My sheep listen to My voice, and I know them, and they follow Me" (John 10:27, NASB).

The Lord has never spoken to me audibly, but he definitely speaks to my heart and mind as I spend time with him in prayer. This communication often occurs in the spiritual realm between God and his Holy Spirit who lives in each Christian.

And when the God of the universe speaks to you, be sure to write it down in your spiritual journal, as Habakkuk 2:2 indicates. A wise Christian maintains a spiritual journal, recording their prayer requests and God's answers. Look for consistency in determining God's will. In summary, spend quality time with the Lord in prayer, sensing God's specific will in managing the money he has entrusted to you.

5. Study God's Word

If we regularly and prayerfully read the Bible, God will speak to us through his word. Psalm 119:105 says, "Your word is a lamp for my feet, a light on my path."

God's word is such an important tool for discerning his will. In Deuteronomy 6:6–9, the Lord admonished his people:

These commandments that I give you today are to be on your hearts. Impress them on your children. Talk about them when you sit at home and when you walk along the road, when you lie down and when you get up. Tie them as symbols on your hands and bind them on your foreheads. Write them on the doorframes of your houses and on your gates.

Clearly, God instructs us to habitually study his word in order to understand his ways in all areas of life, including managing money. If you want to be a faithful steward, you must study and implement God's word on finances.

6. Change the Way You Think

In order for us to manage the money and material things God has entrusted to us in a way that pleases him, we often have to change our thinking. In Romans 12:2, Paul instructed us, "Do not conform any longer to the pattern of this world, but be transformed by the renewing of your mind."

How do you renew your mind? Joshua 1:8 answers, "Keep this Book of the Law always on your lips; meditate on it day and night, so that you may be careful to do everything written in it. Then you will be prosperous and successful."

And why should we meditate on God's word? Hebrews 4:12 says, "The word of God is alive and active. Sharper than any double-edged sword, it penetrates even to dividing soul and spirit, joints and marrow; it judges the thoughts and attitudes of the heart."

In summary, habitually meditate on God's word in the area of finances in order to develop a godly mindset with respect to money and material things.

7. God Can Direct Through Godly Advisers

God can provide specific direction in many ways—by answering our prayers, prompting us by his word, or through the counsel of a godly financial adviser. Although a non-Christian adviser can give good, practical advice, only a spiritually mature Christian will provide biblically based financial advice.

As 1 Corinthians 2:14–15 says:

The person without the Spirit does not accept the things that come from the Spirit of God but considers them foolishness, and cannot understand them because they are discerned only through the Spirit. The person with the Spirit makes judgments about all things, but such a person is not subject to merely human judgments.

In my view, a godly financial adviser who is a spiritually mature Christian has these four qualities:

1. This person understands and applies God's financial principles (Psalm 111:10).
2. He or she has a close personal relationship with the Lord (John 15).
3. This person has the necessary practical financial knowledge (Proverbs 24:3–4).
4. He or she habitually puts the interests of clients first (Philippians 2:3–4).

In summary, before making any major financial decision, seek God's will through prayer and the study of his word, and seek counsel from godly financial advisers.

8. Remember, You Are a Steward, Not an Owner

As you prayerfully ask God for his wisdom (James 1:5) and his specific direction (Psalm 25:12) in managing money, be sure to habitually acknowledge in your heart and mind that you are a steward, not an owner of the money and material things God has entrusted to you.

Haggai 2:8 says, "'The silver is mine and the gold is mine,' declares the LORD Almighty." And Psalm 24:1 says, "The earth is the LORD's, and everything in it." As Paul said in 1 Corinthians 2:16, be sure to have "the mind of Christ," and be willing to use God's money in accordance with his will, not your personal desires (Luke 22:42).

In summary, in order to discern God's will in managing money, habitually acknowledge in your heart and mind that you are a steward of God's resources, and follow his will, not your will.

9. Discerning God's Will

In Judges 6:37–40, Gideon set out a fleece in order to determine God's will. Similarly, subject to prayer and the guidelines provided in Scripture, Christians today should ask God to open and close the appropriate doors so we can discern his will.

Sometimes God will direct us by providing unique opportunities or removing some options. However, be careful. The availability of financing may be not an open door from God but rather a temptation from Satan to get into debt.

Remember, the Lord discouraged debt (Proverbs 22:7). The pattern throughout Scripture is for God to meet needs without creating debt (Deuteronomy 28; Philippians 4:19). In Psalm 32:8, God promised, "I will instruct you and teach you in the way you should go; I will counsel you with my loving eye on you."

In summary, prayerfully ask God to direct you in making financial decisions by opening and closing the appropriate doors.

10. Do You Have God's Peace?

Before making any major financial decisions, you should spend considerable time in prayer, study God's word, and obtain godly counsel. Then you should ask this question: "Is God giving me his peace or lack of peace regarding this proposed financial decision?"

Why? Because when you are in God's will, you will experience God's peace. Jesus said in John 14:27, "Peace I leave with you; my peace I give you. I do not give to you as the world gives." And in Philippians 4:6–7, Paul told us that prayer and a thankful heart will result in "the peace of God, which transcends all understanding."

With respect to managing finances, if you have God's peace, then you are likely in his will. But if you do not have God's peace, then you should prayerfully ask him to reveal his will to you.

11. Stepping Out in Faith

Jordan decided "to step out in faith" by purchasing a house and trusting God for the mortgage payments. After two years, Jordan tracked all of his expenses and realized that the expenses exceeded his income, resulting in additional debt and stress.

Jordan could not understand why God allowed this to happen because he believed that he had stepped out in faith. Unfortunately, Jordan unknowingly violated several biblical principles. For example, in the parable of the tower (Luke 14:28–30), God admonished us to plan ahead, which practically requires the preparation of a budget. Had Jordan done so, he would have realized he could not afford the house before he purchased it.

Based on God's word, a Christian should step out in faith only after doing these things:

1. Seeking God's wisdom (James 1:5) and specific direction (Psalm 32:8).
2. Studying the applicable Scriptures (Psalm 119:105).
3. Obtaining biblically based financial advice (1 Corinthians 2:14–15).
4. Preparing a budget to ensure that you can afford the new expense (Proverbs 21:5).

5. Prayerfully sensing God's peace (John 14:27) with respect to the particular financial decision.

Go to www.coplandfinancialministries.org to learn more about God's word on finances. We have numerous resources there, most of which are free. You can also follow @biblefinance on Facebook, Instagram, and Twitter.

VI.
PRIORITIES

1. Right Priorities Lead to True Riches

Christians often erroneously assume there is no connection between spirituality and money management. But in Luke 16:11, Jesus says, "So if you have not been trustworthy in handling worldly wealth, who will trust you with true riches?" This means our management of money affects the extent to which God provides his true riches.

"True riches" means things that are important to God. These riches include the following three things:

1. A close personal relationship with the Lord. In Philippians 3:8, Paul said, "I consider everything a loss because of the surpassing worth of knowing Christ Jesus my Lord."

2. God's peace. He has promised his peace when we are directed by his Spirit. As Romans 8:6 says, "The mind governed by the flesh is death, but the mind governed by the Spirit is life and peace."

3. God's joy. As indicated in Psalm 16:11, God will provide his joy when we are in his presence. "You make known to me the path of life; you will fill me with joy in your presence, with eternal pleasures at your right hand."

So, according to Scripture, having the right priorities in handling money will enhance our relationship with God. In doing so, we will also experience his peace and joy.

2. Money Competes With God

In Matthew 6:24, Jesus communicated clearly that money can compete with our relationship with God. "No one can serve two masters. Either you will hate the one and love the other, or you will be devoted to the one and despise the other. You cannot serve both God and money."

For example, if people spend more than they earn, they will accumulate debt and experience financial problems. The resulting stress will cause them to focus their time and energy on their financial problems, rather than their relationship with God.

The anxiety will result in a lack of peace, and this will negatively affect their relationship with God. Jesus said, "Where your treasure is, there your heart will be also" (Matthew 6:21). In summary, faithful stewardship of the money God has entrusted to you will enable you to enjoy God's true riches—which include a close personal relationship with the Lord, his joy, and his peace.

3. Good Money Management Builds Treasure in Heaven

Jesus said, "Do not store up for yourselves treasures on earth, where moths and vermin destroy, and where thieves break in and steal. But store up for yourselves treasures in heaven, where moths and vermin do not destroy, and where thieves do not break in and steal" (Matthew 6:19–20).

Treasures on earth include money and material things. We prize such things during our lifetime here on earth, but they will have no importance when we get to heaven. Treasures in heaven include things that will be important when we get to heaven, such as our salvation (which will last for eternity) and the rewards God promises to faithful stewards (Matthew 19:29).

Scripture does not explicitly describe heavenly rewards. However, it's clear that what we do on earth affects what awaits us in heaven. "Godliness has value for all things, holding promise for both the present life and the life to come" (1 Timothy 4:8). Godliness includes the way we manage our finances. Following God's principles for handling money is building treasure in heaven.

4. Financial Faithfulness Has Eternal Value

God's word links financial management to eternal rewards. In 1 Timothy 6:18–19, Paul said, "Command them to do good, to be rich in good deeds, and to be generous and willing to share. In this way they will lay up treasure for themselves as a firm foundation for the coming age, so that they may take hold of the life that is truly life."

In the parable of the talents, eternal rewards are given by God as a result of faithful financial stewardship. Jesus admonished us not to store up treasures on earth but rather to store up treasures in heaven (Matthew 6:19–21).

It's easy to get focused on money and material things. However, since these things are temporary, the wise Christian focuses on treasures in heaven. Colossians 3:2 states, "Set your minds on things above, not on earthly things."

I encourage you to prayerfully ask God to show you how you need to adjust your focus from treasures on earth to treasures in heaven.

5. Financial Character Affects Ministry

An individual's character and resulting management of money can significantly influence their ministry effectiveness. In Luke 16:10, Jesus said, "Whoever can be trusted with very little can also be trusted with much."

In other words, we must first demonstrate the godly character of faithfulness in a small amount before God will entrust us with more.

Secondly, as Jesus said in Luke 16:11, "If you have not been trustworthy in handling worldly wealth, who will trust you with true riches?"

In other words, if we are not trustworthy in handling something of less importance, such as money and material things, then why would God entrust us with the true riches—which includes a close relationship with God and an effective ministry blessed by God.

In summary, we must faithfully manage money according to God's principles and God's will, before we can enjoy a close personal relationship with the Lord and an effective ministry blessed by God.

6. Godly Leadership Requires Biblical Financial Management

A Christian's management of money is often not considered a prerequisite for spiritual leadership. This is unfortunate because God instructs us to ensure that spiritual leaders should manage money God's way.

For example, 1 Timothy 3 says a church elder must *not* be a "lover of money" and "must manage his own family well." This would include managing family finances in a godly fashion. Further, 1 Timothy 3:5 asks this question: "If anyone does not know how to manage his own family, how can he take care of God's church?"

And in Luke 16:11, Jesus said that being untrustworthy with worldly wealth influences whether you will be entrusted with true riches. Since some biblical scholars interpret true riches to include spiritual responsibilities, we can conclude that one prerequisite for spiritual leadership is faithfulness in managing money according to God's principles and God's will.

In summary, a godly spiritual leader must manage money in accordance with God's principles and God's will.

7. Management of Finances Reveals Priorities

Although most Christians say they put God first, their bank accounts often indicate otherwise. Consider the following questions.

1. Do you give God the firstfruits, or does he get the leftovers? Proverbs 3:9–10 states, "Honor the LORD with your wealth, with the firstfruits of all your crops; then your barns will be filled to overflowing, and your vats will brim over with new wine."
2. Do you buy things you really don't need? In Matthew 6:31–33, God promised to meet our needs but not necessarily our wants and desires.
3. Are you spending more than you earn and accumulating debt?
4. Have you developed and implemented a budget? In his illustration of building a tower in Luke 14, Jesus admonished us to plan ahead. A budget is an effective tool for planning your finances.

In reality, one's management of money is a reflection of one's true priorities. I recommend reviewing your expenditures and asking the question: What are my real priorities?

8. Financial Attitudes Are Important

An individual's attitude in the area of finances affects that person's happiness. Consider these questions as a thermometer to test your financial attitudes.

1. Does your spending reflect selfishness, or does it demonstrate personal sacrifice? In Philippians 2:3–4, Paul challenged us not to be selfish.
2. Do you feel envious of what other people have materially? Exodus 20:17 warns against coveting our neighbour's possessions.
3. Do you constantly want more, or are you content with God's provision? Hebrews 13:5 instructs us to avoid getting caught up in the love of money, but to be content with our resources.
4. Do you believe money and material things will bring happiness and peace of mind? In John 14:27, God explained that happiness and peace can only be obtained through a close personal relationship with Jesus Christ.

I encourage you to spend quality time in prayer, asking God to reveal and help you deal with any financial attitudes that need to be changed.

9. Seek God's Direction and Wait for the Lord's Provision
Consider the following questions.

1. Do you borrow money without consulting God? In Proverbs 22:7, God warned that those who borrow money may become a servant to the lender.
2. When you have a material need, do you pray and wait patiently for God to provide? "Rest in the Lord and wait patiently for Him" (Psalm 37:7, NASB).
3. Or do you just make the purchase, perhaps on credit, without giving God a chance to meet that need? In Matthew 6:31–33, God promised he will meet our needs as we put him first in all aspects of life, including managing money.

4. Do you spend quality time in prayer and reading God's word before making major financial decisions? In Isaiah 48:17, God made a wonderful promise. "I am the LORD your God, who teaches you what is best for you, who directs you in the way you should go."

In summary, before making any major financial decision, be sure to seek God's specific direction through prayer, reading his word, and waiting patiently for the Lord's provision.

10. Build Your Finances on the Rock of God's Word

The Bible contains phenomenal wisdom on finances. But unfortunately, most Christians either have a limited understanding of God's financial principles, or they haven't implemented God's truths regarding managing money.

For those who have implemented God's truths, Christ said in Matthew 7:24–25:

"Therefore everyone who hears these words of mine and puts them into practice is like a wise man who built his house on the rock. The rain came down, the streams rose, and the winds blew and beat against that house; yet it did not fall, because it had its foundation on the rock."

But to those who are not managing money God's way, Christ warned, "Everyone who hears these words of mine and does not put them into practice is like a foolish man who built his house on sand. The rain came down, the streams rose, and the winds blew and beat against that house, and it fell with a great crash" (Matthew 7:26–27).

In summary, if we manage money God's way, we will be blessed. But if we don't manage money God's way, we will suffer the consequences.

93

Go to www.coplandfinancialministries.org to learn more about God's word on finances. We have numerous resources there, most of which are free. You can also follow @biblefinance on Facebook, Instagram, and Twitter.

VII.
WORLDLY VERSUS BIBLICAL PERSPECTIVES ON MONEY

1. Christians Can Have a Worldly Perspective on Money

Do you think there is a difference between a non-Christian perspective and a biblical perspective when it comes to managing money and material things? Well, the answer is yes, there is a difference.

The biblical truth is that there is a tremendous difference between a non-Christian and a biblical perspective. During the next several financial moments, I will provide examples of those differences.

Do you think Christians ever fall into the non-Christian mindset?

Yes, sometimes Christians unintentionally or unknowingly manage money in a worldly manner. This mindset can be changed by studying the Bible and gaining a more thorough understanding of what it says about finances.

As you reflect on these questions, I encourage you to pray as David did in Psalm 139:23–24. "Search me, God, and know my heart; test me and know my anxious thoughts. See if there is any offensive way in me, and lead me in the way everlasting."

2. God Owns It All

There is a big difference between what the world teaches and a biblical perspective on money and material things. For example, most people believe they own their material resources and therefore can spend their money as they wish—often spending it on selfish desires.

However, the absolute truth is we are managing the money and material things God has entrusted to us while we're here on earth. The split second after you die, you will likely realize you are not an owner, just a steward of God's resources.

Ecclesiastes 5:15 states, "Everyone comes naked from their mother's womb, and as everyone comes, so they depart. They take nothing from their toil that they can carry in their hands."

The biblical perspective is to acknowledge in your heart and mind that God owns everything and look to him and his word as to how we should use his money. Haggai 2:8 states, "'The silver is mine and the gold is mine,' declares the LORD Almighty."

3. Look to God and His Word

Here is another difference between a worldly perspective versus a biblical perspective on managing money. The worldly perspective is to look to oneself and the wisdom of this world for direction in managing money.

This worldly wisdom has caused many people to spend more than they earn, accumulate debt, and later suffer the consequences. Yet Psalm 1:1–2 states: "Blessed is the one who does not walk in step with the wicked or stand in the way that sinners take or sit in the company of mockers, but whose delight is in the law of the LORD, and who meditates on his law day and night."

The biblical approach is to look to God and his word for direction in using money. James 1:5 says: "If any of you lacks wisdom, you should ask God, who gives generously to all without finding fault, and it will be given to you. But when you ask you must believe and not doubt."

In summary, we need to look to God and his word for direction in using the financial resources he has entrusted to us.

4. Give God the Firstfruits

Christians with a worldly perspective on money will typically give God the leftovers. These leftovers are usually small.

In 2 Corinthians 9:6–7, Paul said, "Remember this: Whoever sows sparingly will also reap sparingly, and whoever sows generously will also reap generously. Each of you should give what you have decided in your heart to give, not reluctantly or under compulsion, for God loves a cheerful giver."

On the other hand, a committed Christian managing money God's way will make giving to God's work a very high priority. That is, they will give God the firstfruits of their income, which is consistent with God's word.

Proverbs 3:9–10 states, "Honor the LORD with your wealth, with the firstfruits of all your crops; then your barns will be filled to overflowing, and your vats will brim over with new wine."

Therefore, as Christians, we need to give God our firstfruits, not our leftovers.

5. Contentment Is Great Gain

An individual with a worldly perspective on money and material things is generally more discontent with their current level of income and frequently wants more and more. This contrasts with what Hebrews 13:5 says, "Keep your lives free from the love of money and be content with what you have, because God has said, 'Never will I leave you; never will I forsake you.'"

In Luke 3:14, John the Baptist admonished some soldiers, telling them: "Don't extort money and don't accuse people falsely—be content with your pay." Most people struggle with discontent, selfishness, covetousness, or pride causing them to want more money and material things.

The biblical solution to this thinking is to learn to be content with God's provision. How important is contentment from God's perspective? Paul answered this in 1 Timothy 6:6–8. "Godliness with contentment is great gain. For we brought nothing into the world, and we can take nothing out of it. But if we have food and clothing, we will be content with that."

In summary, be content with God's provision so you can have a biblical perspective on money and material things.

6. Trust God to Provide

An individual with a worldly perspective on money often struggles with fear of the future or of losing assets. God provides some comfort to those of his children who manage money his way. "Have no fear of sudden disaster or of the ruin that overtakes the wicked, for the LORD will be at your side and will keep your foot from being snared" (Proverbs 3:25–26).

A person with a biblical perspective on money doesn't fear, but rather trusts God to meet their needs. As Proverbs 3:5–6 states, "Trust in the LORD with all your heart and lean not on your own understanding; in all your ways submit to him, and he will make your paths straight."

And in Matthew 6:31–33, Jesus said:

> "Do not worry, saying, 'What shall we eat?' or 'What shall we drink?' or 'What shall we wear?' For the pagans run after all these things, and your heavenly Father knows that you need them. But seek first his kingdom and his righteousness, and all these things will be given to you as well."

In summary, do not fear. Rather, put God first, and trust him to meet your needs.

7. We Are Accountable to God

People with a worldly perspective on money often believe they aren't accountable to anyone outside of their close human relationships. In other words, they believe they can use their money as they wish.

On the other hand, committed Christians with a biblical perspective on money understand we are stewards of the money and material things God has entrusted to us. Since we believe this, we know we're accountable to the Lord. In Romans 14:12, Paul said, "So then, each of us will give an account of ourselves to God."

In Matthew 25, Jesus told a story of a master (who represents God) who entrusted five talents to one servant, two to another, and one to the third servant. After a long time (perhaps a lifetime?) God returned and made each servant accountable for 100 per cent of what he had entrusted to them.

In summary, we are each individually accountable to God for how we use all the resources he has entrusted to us.

8. Use Money for Eternal Purposes

Someone with a worldly perspective on money will typically use money to buy things that are treasures on earth. Jesus said, "Do not store up for yourselves treasures on earth, where moths and vermin destroy, and where thieves break in and steal. But store up for yourselves treasures in heaven where moths and vermin do not destroy, and where thieves do not break in and steal" (Matthew 6:19–20).

Christians with a biblical perspective on money will intentionally use money for eternal purposes.

1 Timothy 6:17–19 states:

Command those who are rich in this present world not to be arrogant nor to put their hope in wealth, which is so uncertain, but to put their hope in God, who richly provides us with everything for our enjoyment. Command them to do good, to be rich in good deeds, and to be generous and willing to share. In this way they will lay up treasure for themselves as a firm foundation for the coming age, so that they may take hold of the life that is truly life.

In summary, Christians need to build up treasures in heaven by using money for their needs or the needs of others and giving generously to God's work.

9. Money and Talents Come from God

Those with a worldly perspective on money believe their financial successes are due to their hard work alone. In other words, they made it happen. God disagrees. Deuteronomy 8:17–18 states, "You may say to yourself, 'My power and the strength of my hands have produced this wealth for me.' But remember the LORD your God, for it is he who gives you the ability to produce wealth."

In other words, all of our natural abilities come from God. As for committed Christians who have a biblical perspective on money, they thank God for the talents and abilities God has provided, including the gift of earning an above-average income.

As 1 Chronicles 29:12–13 states, "Wealth and honor come from you; you are the ruler of all things. In your hands are strength and power to exalt and give strength to all. Now, our God, we give you thanks, and praise your glorious name."

In summary, we must acknowledge and thank God for the money and natural abilities he has provided us with.

10. Avoid a Get-Rich-Quick Mindset

Someone with a worldly perspective on money may look for opportunities to get rich quickly. God warned against this in Proverbs 23:4–5, which states, "Do not wear yourself out to get rich; do not trust your own cleverness. Cast but a glance at riches, and they are gone, for they will surely sprout wings and fly off to the sky like an eagle."

Committed Christians with a biblical perspective on money don't try to get rich quickly. Instead, they but work faithfully wherever God has directed them.

Proverbs 28:19–20 states, "Those who work their land will have abundant food, but those who chase fantasies will have their fill of poverty. A faithful person will be richly blessed, but one eager to get rich will not go unpunished." The concept of "working one's land" implies that we should focus on investing our time and money in the areas that we understand.

In summary, a committed Christian does not try to get rich quickly, but rather works diligently and invests in areas they understand.

11. Learn to Be Content

A person with a worldly perspective on money often struggles with wanting what other people have. In Deuteronomy 5:21, God commands, "You shall not covet your neighbor's wife. You shall not set your desire on your neighbor's house or land, his male or female servant, his ox or donkey, or anything that belongs to your neighbor."

Clearly, God doesn't want Christians to have covetous attitudes toward money and material things. Committed Christians shouldn't covet what other people have. Rather, they should be content with God's provision and follow Paul's instructions in Philippians 4:11–13:

> I have learned to be content whatever the circumstances. I know what it is to be in need, and I know what it is to have plenty. I have learned the secret of being content in any and every situation, whether well fed or hungry, whether living in plenty or in want. I can do all this through him who gives me strength.

Paul's secret was his close relationship with Jesus Christ and his focus on things of eternal value (Colossians 3:1–2) rather than temporal things.

In summary, depending upon God, we need to learn to be content with his provisions and not covet what other people have.

12. Provide for the Needs of Your Family

People with a worldly perspective on money and material things will often either neglect the needs of their family or spoil them without healthy boundaries. When someone neglects the needs of their family, especially immediate family, 1 Timothy 5:8 states that this person "has denied the faith and is worse than an unbeliever."

When parents spoil their kids by buying them a lot of things they don't need, they are unintentionally teaching their children an unwise perspective on money. This results in their kids expecting to live a lifestyle that may be greater than what they can afford, which can lead to all kinds of financial and marital problems in the future.

However, Christians who have a biblical perspective on money will focus on providing for the needs of the family. They may provide other wants and desires within reason and will teach their kids financial responsibility and hard work. Proverbs 22:6 states, "Start children off on the way they should go, and even when they are old they will not turn from it."

In summary, provide for the needs of your family, but don't spoil them.

13. Developing Godly Character Traits

The typical character traits of those with a worldly perspective on money and material things include selfishness, covetousness, fear, pride, greed, dishonesty, trusting oneself, the love of money, unrighteous, and frustration.

These traits are clearly contrary to God's word. As for the committed Christian who has a biblical perspective, their typical character traits are humility, generosity, faithfulness, honesty, contentment, righteousness, peace, love for the Lord, and trust in him.

Many of these godly characteristics are consistent with Paul's definition of the fruits of the spirit in Galatians 5:22–23. "The fruit of the Spirit is love, joy, peace, forbearance, kindness, goodness, faithfulness, gentleness and self-control. Against such things there is no law."

In summary, we need to develop a biblical perspective on money and demonstrate godly characteristics in how we manage money.

14. Case Study One: A Worldly Perspective on Money

Susan is a Christian who believes the money she earns is hers because she works hard for it. Therefore, she can spend her money however she wishes—often on things that are superfluous wants and desires. Susan gives very little to God's work and has never studied God's word on finances.

Because of this limited knowledge, Susan is not aware of Deuteronomy 8:17–18, which states, "You may say to your-self, 'My power and the strength of my hands have produced this wealth for me.' But remember the LORD your God, for it is he who gives you the ability to produce wealth."

Susan clearly has a worldly perspective on money. She needs to understand that God owns everything; Susan is merely a steward of what God has entrusted to him (Haggai 2:8).

Do you, perhaps unknowingly, have a worldly perspective on money?

15. Case Study Two: A Biblical Perspective on Money

Jean is a committed Christian who has done an in-depth study of what God's word says about finances. She acknowledges that God is the owner of everything and that we are stewards or managers of what he has entrusted to us.

Jean often quotes Psalm 24:1, which states: "The earth is the LORD's, and everything in it."

Jean has learned to be content (Philippians 4:11–13) and to live within God's provision. She has implemented a budget (Luke 14:28–30) to ensure she spends less than she earns so she can pay off debts and save for future needs.

As a result, today Jean has little debt and is able to generously give well over 10 per cent of her income to God's work. Jean regu-larly asks God for his wisdom (James 1:5) and specific direction (Psalm 32:8) in managing the money God has entrusted to her. Clearly, Jean has a biblical perspective on money.

Do you have a biblical perspective or an unbiblical perspec-tive on money?

16. Bernard and Judy Accumulate Debt

Here is a common situation I've seen thousands of times. Bernard and Judy are a typical middle-class family. They purchased a house 20 years ago, but over the years they spent more than they earned. On several occasions, they obtained a line of credit on their home in order to pay off their credit cards and other debts.

As a result, the mortgage and the line of credit on their home is greater today than the original cost of their house two decades ago. In other words, they used the increased value of their home to finance a lifestyle they could not afford. Now they are stressed out about finances.

With credit so readily available, Bernard and Judy's situation is very common, but it is contrary to God's word. God discouraged debt (Proverbs 22:7) and admonished us to plan and save for future needs (Proverbs 21:20). This involves paying down all debts, including your mortgage. If Bernard and Judy had managed money God's way, they should have no mortgage after 20 years.

17. An Example of Biblical Stewardship

Shortly after Fraser accepted Christ, he studied and meditated on what God's word said with respect to finances. Fraser acknowledged that God owns everything and that he is a steward of the money the Lord has entrusted to him. Depending upon God for wisdom and direction, Fraser applied biblical principles in managing money.

He developed and implemented a budget to ensure he spent less than he earned. Even though he had accumulated significant debt previously, in faith he gave the first 10 per cent of his income to God's work. God blessed and enabled him to pay off all his debts within three years!

Fraser learned to be content with a lifestyle that was less than his income; he saved a good down payment and bought a home. He is currently paying down his mortgage quickly, and he should be debt-free in ten years. Fraser praises God for his wisdom in the Bible.

18. A Worldly Perspective on Investing

Steve believes the Bible says nothing about investing. Instead, he relies only on the comments of well-known investment advisers who appear in the media. Steve wants to make a lot of money, so he borrows to invest. However, during market downturns, he incurs significant losses and becomes stressed out.

Steve has a worldly perspective on investing. He is unaware of the many passages in the Bible that apply to investing, and has violated these investment principles.

In Deuteronomy 28, God promised his people if they fully obeyed him, they would be a lender and not a borrower. The emphasis in Scripture is to save a little at a time (Proverbs 13:11) over a long period of time. "Steady plodding brings prosperity; hasty speculation brings poverty" (Proverbs 21:5, TLB).

Steve should implement a budget (Luke 14:28–30) so he has a surplus each month. He can then invest gradually in a diversified portfolio in accordance with Ecclesiastes 11:2.

To learn more about what God's word says about investing, go to the section of this book titled "Investing God's Way."

19. Biblical Perspective on Investing

Bill has studied what the Bible says about investing. He prays and asks God to provide his wisdom (James 1:5) and direction

(Psalm 25:12) for investing the money God has entrusted to him. Bill does not borrow to invest because the Bible discourages debt (Proverbs 22:7) and because God promised his people that if they fully obey him, God would bless them and provide for their needs (Deuteronomy 28:1–14).

In addition, Bill doesn't try to make a lot of money quickly, but rather he invests a little at a time over a long period of time. "The plans of the diligent lead surely to abundance, but everyone who is hasty comes only to poverty" (Proverbs 21:5, ESV).

To accomplish this, Bill has implemented a budget to ensure he has a surplus each month to invest in future needs such as retirement and children's education. During downturns in the market, Bill meditates on Scriptures such as Matthew 6:31–33. These truths reassure him that God will provide for his needs, notwithstanding bad market conditions.

20. Summary of Worldly and Biblical Perspectives on Money

There is a tremendous difference between worldly and biblical perspectives on money and material things. Unfortunately, sometimes Christians fall into the worldly mindset. Generally speaking, Christians with a biblical perspective on money act in the following ways.

1. They acknowledge that God owns everything and that they are stewards of God's resources (1 Chronicles 29:11–14).
2. They habitually pray and ask God for his wisdom (James 1:5) and direction (Psalm 32:8) in managing money.
3. They make giving to God's work a priority (Proverbs 3:9–10).

4. They are content to live within God's provision (1 Timothy 6:6–8).

5. They put God first and trust him to meet their needs (Matthew 6:31–33).

6. They understand that they are individually accountable to God as to how they use the resources they've been given (Romans 14:12).

7. They use money for eternal purposes (1 Timothy 6:17–19).

8. They thank God often for what they have (Psalm 118:1) rather than complaining about what they don't have.

The Bible has so much wisdom on managing money. I encourage you to visit www.coplandfinancialministries.org, and study the numerous resources. As you learn and apply God's word in the area of finances, God will meet your needs and provide you with his wisdom and direction. Then you will eventually experience God's peace in the area of finances.

VIII.
COUNSEL AND WISDOM

1. God Provides Financial Wisdom

When dealing with important financial decisions, we must obtain wisdom and counsel from God. Job 12:13 says, "To God belong wisdom and power; counsel and understanding are his." Isaiah described God's counsel as wonderful and magnificent (Isaiah 28:29).

How does the Lord provide his financial wisdom? Generally, God will direct us through Bible verses that provide his wisdom in a particular situation. Here are three examples:

1. In the parable of the tower (Luke 14:28–30), Christ admonished us to plan ahead.
2. God warned of the dangers of debt (Proverbs 22:7).
3. God instructed us to give him the firstfruits of our income (Proverbs 3:9–10).

God provides incredible financial wisdom in his word, but unfortunately, very few people use it.

In summary, to properly deal with any important financial decision, first seek God's wisdom by prayerfully studying his word on finances. Psalm 119:105 says, "Your word is a lamp for my feet, a light on my path."

2. Seek God's Wisdom and Specific Direction

Too often, we believe we have to figure things out on our own. But God wants us to seek his wisdom and counsel on any important decision. As 1 Kings 22:5 tells us, "First seek the counsel of the LORD."

If you want God's financial wisdom, the starting point is to have the utmost respect for God—that is, the fear of God. Proverbs 9:10 states, "The fear of the LORD is the beginning of wisdom, and knowledge of the Holy One is understanding." If you don't have a personal relationship with God (in other words, "knowledge of the Holy One"), then you will never be able to access true financial wisdom.

If you do have a personal relationship with Jesus Christ, then you must study his word for his financial principles and spend quality time with the Lord in prayer, listening to his voice for specific direction. Jesus said, "My sheep listen to my voice; I know them, and they follow me" (John 10:27).

3. God Will Direct Us

Are you facing an important financial decision? If yes, then here are some suggestions.

First, search God's word for financial wisdom. Often, the Lord provides his directives within his word. Again, Psalm 119:105 says, "Your word is a lamp for my feet, a light on my path."

However, sometimes the Bible doesn't provide specific instruction for a particular situation. When this occurs, then you should spend quality time with the Lord in prayer. Jeremiah 29:11–13 says:

> "I know the plans I have for you," declares the LORD, "plans to prosper you and not to harm you, plans to give you hope and a future. Then you will call on me and come and pray to me, and I will listen to you. You will seek me and find me when you seek me with all your heart."

Clearly, God has a plan, and if we pray and seek him with all our hearts, then the Lord will listen and provide his instructions.

In summary, through prayer and studying of God's word, develop a close relationship with the Lord so you can sense his specific will for your life.

4. God's Word Provides Much Financial Wisdom

With 16 parables from Christ and more than 2,300 references referring to money and material things, God's word contains tremendous financial wisdom.

How important is God's word? It's so important that God instructed Joshua, "Keep this Book of the Law always on your lips; meditate on it day and night, so that you may be careful to do everything written in it. Then you will be prosperous and successful" (Joshua 1:8).

How powerful is God's word? Hebrews 4:12 answers, "The word of God is alive and active. Sharper than any double-edged sword, it penetrates even to dividing soul and spirit, joints and marrow; it judges the thoughts and attitudes of the heart."

This is amazing. God, through his word and Spirit, judges the thoughts and the attitudes of our hearts, including our motives when it comes to money and material things. How applicable is God's word? "All Scripture is God-breathed and is useful for teaching, rebuking, correcting and training in righteousness, so that the servant of God may be thoroughly equipped for every good work" (2 Timothy 3:16–17).

In summary, I encourage you to habitually study God's word on finances to ensure that you are managing money God's way.

5. Following God's Financial Principles Is Essential

When people get into financial difficulty, it is generally because they have violated God's financial principles, often unknowingly. Here are four examples of not following God's wisdom:

1. Having no savings for an emergency. Proverbs 21:20 says those who are wise save for the future.
2. Taking on too much debt. God's word warned of the dangers of debt in Proverbs 22:7.
3. Co-signing a loan. In Proverbs 17:18, the Bible advises against this.
4. A worldly attitude with respect to money, such as covetousness or selfishness. The Bible warns against these attitudes in Exodus 20:17 and Philippians 2:3–4.

Almost always, the financial problems can be avoided by simply following the counsel and wisdom of the Bible. Psalm 119:105 says, "Your word is a lamp for my feet, a light on my path."

God promises great blessings to those who manage money his way. "Blessed are those who keep his statutes and seek him with all their heart" (Psalm 119:2). If you want to experience God's blessings in the area of finances, you need to follow his financial principles.

6. Obtain Counsel

God instructs us to obtain biblical counsel. Proverbs 12:15 states, "The way of fools seems right to them, but the wise listen to advice." Sometimes Christians don't seek financial counsel. This could be for various reasons, including pride. Proverbs 13:10 states, "Where there is strife, there is pride, but wisdom is found in those who take advice."

God indicates our probability of success is greater with many advisers. Proverbs 15:22 says, "Plans fail for lack of counsel, but with many advisers they succeed." After obtaining counsel, it is our responsibility to pray and ask God to give us his wisdom in weighing the advice. "The simple believe anything, but the prudent give thought to their steps" (Proverbs 14:15).

In summary, for any important financial decision, obtain counsel from several godly advisers, weigh the advice, and above all, "seek the counsel of the LORD" (1 Kings 22:5).

7. Seek Advice from Godly Financial Advisers

Be sure to seek financial advice from godly financial advisers. As 1 Corinthians 2:14 tells us, "The person without the Spirit does not accept the things that come from the Spirit of God but considers them foolishness, and cannot understand them because they are discerned only through the Spirit."

Although a non-Christian could give some good, practical advice, only a spiritually mature Christian will provide biblically based financial advice.

For example, a non-believer likely will not understand a Christian's desire to give generously to God's work. The Christian has an eternal perspective, wanting to build up "treasures in heaven," while the non-believer has a temporal perspective, wanting to build up "treasures on earth" (Matthew 6:19–21).

In addition, a godly adviser would counsel you to use minimal debt, while many worldly advisers would encourage the use of significant debt (Proverbs 22:7). "Blessed is the man who walks not in the counsel of the ungodly" (Psalm 1:1, NKJV).

In conclusion, before making a major financial decision, seek counsel from spiritually mature, godly financial advisers.

8. A Definition of a Godly Financial Adviser

I recommend that you seek the advice of two or three godly advisers before you make any major financial decision. Here's my definition of a godly financial adviser.

A godly financial adviser would be a spiritually mature Christian who understands and applies God's financial principles (Psalm

111:10), has a close personal relationship with God (John 15), has the necessary practical financial knowledge (Proverbs 24:3–4), and habitually puts the interests of clients first (Philippians 2:3–4).

In addition, one of your counsellors should be your spouse, even if they have limited financial knowledge. God, through his Holy Spirit, can give his peace or lack of peace (John 14:27) to an objective spouse who isn't emotionally excited about or biased toward a particular decision. And, as indicated in Genesis 2:24, God wants husbands and wives to be unified, which includes unity on important financial decisions.

In summary, seek godly counsel and the counsel of your spouse, and proceed only after God has given you his peace (John 14:27) and wisdom (James 1:5).

9. Trust God to Direct You

John and Susan had saved a reasonable down payment for a home. Before purchasing a house, they decided to seek God's wisdom (Job 12:13) and direction (Psalm 25:12).

As they studied God's word, they realized that only the Lord knows the future (Genesis 41:25–30) and only he is in control (Psalm 103:19). As a result, they prayed daily for God's direction. Through his Spirit and his word, God instructed them not to purchase a home at that time. They obeyed (Deuteronomy 28:1–12) and waited upon the Lord (Psalm 37:7).

Over the next three years, the price of homes decreased significantly. When they prayed about buying a house again, God granted his peace (John 14:27), and they purchased a home. John and Susan paid fifty thousand dollars less for their home and had twenty-five thousand dollars more in savings. This resulted in a mortgage that was seventy-five thousand dollars less than what it would've been three years previously.

What a blessing to wait upon the Lord! Isaiah 48:17 says, "I am the LORD your God, who teaches you what is best for you, who directs you in the way you should go."

10. Discerning God's Direction

In many Scriptures, God promised to direct us. For example, in Psalm 32:8, God said, "I will instruct you and teach you in the way you should go; I will counsel you with my loving eye on you." Here are some ways God instructs us.

1. God can provide his peace or lack thereof regarding a particular financial decision. Jesus said, "Peace I leave with you; my peace I give you" (John 14:27).
2. God will often direct us through his word. "Your word is a lamp for my feet, a light on my path" (Psalm 119:105).
3. God can direct us through godly counsel (Proverbs 12:15).
4. Or, through the Holy Spirit, God can speak to our hearts and minds. Jesus said, "My sheep listen to My voice, and I know them, and they follow Me" (John 10:27, NASB).

Therefore, when facing any important financial decision, prayerfully ask God to direct you according to his will through his word, godly counsel, and his Holy Spirit.

11. Discerning God's Will in Your Circumstances

Can circumstances reveal God's will with respect to financial decisions? The answer is sometimes yes, sometimes no. For example, the availability of credit should not be interpreted as a directive from God to borrow and buy.

Why? Because easy credit creates a tremendous temptation to borrow, while the pattern throughout Scripture is for God to meet our needs without incurring debt (for example, Deuteronomy 28). Further, the Lord warned of the dangers of debt (Proverbs 22:7), and his directive for us is that we save for future needs (Proverbs 21:20) as opposed to borrowing.

Therefore, before you make any major financial decision, make sure that it is the Lord's will (James 4:15). How do we determine the Lord's will?

Firstly, ensure your decision is within biblical financial principles. Secondly, spend quality time with the Lord in prayer, sensing God's specific will. Psalm 25:12 says, "Who is the person who fears the LORD? He will instruct him in the way he should choose."

12. Assessing Biblical Versus Worldly Counsel

Laura is perplexed because of the differing advice she received from two financial advisers who attend her church. Sam recommended she borrow against the equity in her home and invest in several mutual funds, explaining that she could increase her returns with the debt.

However, Tim recommended she not borrow, but rather follow a budget to ensure that she was spending less than she earned and regularly invest her monthly surplus. To determine God's will, Laura studied what the Bible says about finances.

Laura was surprised that the Bible said so much about finances. For example, God discouraged debt (Proverbs 22:7); the Lord promised to meet our needs without debt (Philippians 4:19); and the emphasis in Scripture is to gradually save for future needs as opposed to borrowing (Proverbs 21:20).

In conclusion, do not assume that all Christian financial advisers provide biblically based financial advice. Rather, learn for yourself what God's word says about finances. Unfortunately, many provide financial advice based upon their secular training. In this case, Tim had a good understanding of God's word on finances and provided biblically based financial advice. Nevertheless, there is no substitute for you to learn what God's word says about finances.

Go to www.coplandfinancialministries.org to learn more about God's word on finances. We have numerous resources there, most of which are free. You can also follow @biblefinance on Facebook, Instagram, and Twitter.

IX.
GIVING

1. Give God the Firstfruits, Not the Leftovers

Proverbs 3:9–10 is clear: we should give God the firstfruits of our income. "Honor the LORD with your wealth, with the firstfruits of all your crops; then your barns will be filled to overflowing, and your vats will brim over with new wine."

Unfortunately, in our materialistic society, many Christians do not make it a priority to give to God's work. As a result, God gets the leftovers, which are usually small. But when we give God the firstfruits, we will experience the joy of giving. Jesus said, "It is more blessed to give than to receive" (Acts 20:35).

And in 1 Timothy 6:19, Paul explained the benefits of generous giving. "In this way they will lay up treasure for themselves as a firm foundation for the coming age, so that they may take hold of the life that is truly life."

Therefore, when you prepare your budget and receive your income, habitually give God the firstfruits, not the leftovers.

2. Give Regularly to God's Work

Sometimes, Christians give sporadically to God's work, but this is not God's will. In 1 Corinthians 16:1–2 Paul instructed the Corinthians to give regularly to God's work:

> Now about the collection for the Lord's people: Do what I told the Galatian churches to do. On the first day of every week, each one of you should set aside a sum of money in keeping with your income, saving it up, so that when I come no collections will have to be made.

Like any family or business, God's church and parachurch organizations need income on a regular and consistent basis. Nowhere in Scripture does God encourage deferred giving. Rather, the emphasis is on honouring the Lord with your firstfruits (Proverbs 3:9–10).

And as a practical matter, if you don't give regularly to God's work, you will likely spend the money or hoard it. So, make it a priority to give regularly and consistently to God's work.

3. Give as a Steward, Not an Owner

Haggai 2:8 says, "'The silver is mine and the gold is mine,' declares the LORD Almighty." And Psalm 24:1 reads, "The earth is the LORD's, and everything in it, the world, and all who live in it." In other words, we are stewards or managers of the money the Lord has entrusted to us. God is the owner!

As stewards, we must use God's money according to his will, not our own will. This includes giving generously as the Lord directs. Acknowledging God's ownership of our money is a critical prerequisite to becoming a generous giver. If you believe the money you have is yours to do with as you please, it is unlikely you will ever give generously.

However, if you acknowledge you are a manager of God's resources, and if you love the Lord Jesus Christ and have a close personal relationship with him, then you can learn to give generously with God's help.

4. Consider it a Privilege to Give to God's Work

In 1 Chronicles, King David acknowledged God's sovereignty and power:

"Yours is the mighty power and glory and victory and majesty. Everything in the heavens and earth is yours, O Lord, and this is your kingdom. We adore you as being in control of everything. Riches and honor come from you alone, and you are the ruler of all mankind; your hand controls power and might, and it is at your discretion that men are made great and given strength." (1 Chronicles 29:11–12, TLB)

Our all-powerful God does not need our money to accomplish his work. However, because of his grace, he allows us, as Christians, to participate in his work through giving. Sometimes we consider this a burden. But in reality, it is a privilege and a joy to give to God's work. Jesus said, "It is more blessed to give than to receive" (Acts 20:35).

Never forget, God is the greatest giver of all; he gave us eternal life through his son, Jesus Christ. In summary, consider giving to God's work a privilege and something to be enjoyed.

5. Focus on the Eternal, Not the Temporal
In Matthew 6:19–20, Jesus said:

"Do not store up for yourselves treasures on earth, where moths and vermin destroy, and where thieves break in and steal. But store up for yourselves treasures in heaven, where moths and vermin do not destroy, and where thieves do not break in and steal."

"Treasures on earth" are things that we treasure while here on earth but will be of no value in heaven. This would include using money and material things for selfish and temporary purposes.

On the other hand, "treasures in heaven" represent things that we will treasure in heaven, such as the salvation of people and the rewards God will give us based on our stewardship of money while on earth.

In Matthew 16:27, Jesus said, "The Son of Man is going to come in his Father's glory with his angels, and then he will reward each person according to what they have done."

In summary, manage money and material things with an eternal perspective, not a temporal perspective.

6. Tithing and Free Will Giving

Under Mosaic Law the Jews were required to give three tithes:

1. The Levite tithe (Leviticus 27:30–32).
2. The festival tithe (Deuteronomy 14:22–23).
3. The poor tithe, every three years (Deuteronomy 14:28–29).

So if you are legalistic about tithing, you should give 23.33 per cent of your income to God! However, today we are not under Mosaic Law. If you study the New Testament, the emphasis is to give generously and sacrificially to God's work as a result of your love for the Lord, with no emphasis on percentages. In 2 Corinthians 8:7–8 Paul said:

But since you excel in everything—in faith, in speech, in knowledge, in complete earnestness and in the love we have kindled in you—see that you also excel in this grace of giving. I am not commanding you, but I want to test the sincerity of your love by comparing it with the earnestness of others.

What constitutes generous and sacrificial giving will depend upon each individual's circumstances. For example, a single mom with two kids may be giving generously and sacrificially at

121

5 per cent of her income, while a high-income earner who gives 10 per cent of his income may be giving "out of obedience" but not giving generously.

God instructs us to give generously, from a willing and cheerful heart. As 2 Corinthians 9:6–7 says, "Whoever sows sparingly will also reap sparingly, and whoever sows generously will also reap generously. Each of you should give what you have decided in your heart to give, not reluctantly or under compulsion, for God loves a cheerful giver."

A gift out of love in response to what Christ did for us should not be constrained. Remember Zacchaeus, who as a new Christian immediately gave 50 per cent of all his possessions. This was a tangible reflection of his commitment to the Lord.

In summary, let's give generously and sacrificially to God.

7. Don't Be Constrained by the Tithe
Sometimes, Christians work up to giving 10 per cent of their income to God and stop there even as the Lord continues to bless them. Compared to most people in the world, those of us living in North America are rich. In 1 Timothy 6:17–18, Paul said:

Command those who are rich in this present world not to be arrogant nor to put their hope in wealth, which is so uncertain, but to put their hope in God, who richly provides us with everything for our enjoyment. Command them to do good, to be rich in good deeds, and to be generous and willing to share.

God wants us to be generous. How generous should we be? Jesus said, "From everyone who has been given much, much will be demanded; and from the one who has been entrusted with much, much more will be asked" (Luke 12:48).

Many of us have been entrusted with much, and therefore, God wants us to be very generous. Yes, well beyond the tithe! Remember, we will be held accountable. Romans 14:12 says, "So then, each of us will give an account of ourselves to God." In summary, give generously to God's work, and do not be constrained by the tithe.

8. Give Generously

God encourages generous giving. Jesus said, "Give, and it will be given to you. A good measure, pressed down, shaken together and running over, will be poured into your lap. For with the measure you use, it will be measured to you" (Luke 6:38).

In the parables of the hidden treasure and the fine pearls (Matthew 13:44–46), Christ explained that the kingdom of heaven is of such great value that you should be prepared, if need be, to joyfully give up everything you own to attain it. When Zacchaeus became a new Christian, he was filled with excitement and love for Christ and gave 50 per cent of everything he owned to the poor (Luke 19:8–10).

In light of what God has done for us—providing eternal life through his son, Jesus Christ—how could we, as Christians, not be willing to give generously to God? In summary, as a result of your love for God, give generously to God's work, and he will bless you, both here on earth and for eternity in heaven (Matthew 19:29).

9. God Rewards Generous Givers

Compared to the rest of the world, most of us in the West are rich in material possessions. In 1 Timothy 6:17–18, Paul said:

Command those who are rich in this present world not to be arrogant nor to put their hope in wealth, which is so uncertain, but to put their hope in God, who richly provides us with everything for our enjoyment. Command them to do good, to be rich in good deeds, and to be generous and willing to share.

Why give generously? Paul answered in 1 Timothy 6:19, "In this way they will lay up treasure for themselves as a firm foundation for the coming age, so that they may take hold of the life that is truly life." In other words, give generously to God's work, and you will increase rewards in heaven and the Lord's blessings here on earth.

How significant are God's blessings? In Matthew 19:29, Jesus answers, "Everyone who has left houses or brothers or sisters or father or mother or wife or children or fields for my sake will receive a hundred times as much and will inherit eternal life."

Wow! Think about it—when you give generously to God's work, you will eventually receive one hundred times as much. That means a ten thousand per cent return, and it's all guaranteed by God!

In summary, God will reward generous givers both here on earth and in heaven for eternity!

10. Ensure Your Motives Are Godly and Not Worldly

A Christian can give money to God's work with either worldly motives or godly motives.

Worldly motives include selfishness (expecting to get something in return), manipulation, and pride. In Matthew 6:1–4, Christ challenged the Pharisees' motives as they announced their giving with trumpets so people would honour them.

Here are some examples of godly motives for giving to God's work:

1. Giving out of worship and service God (Luke 4:8).
2. Giving to demonstrate your faith and trust in the Lord (Proverbs 3:5–6).
3. Giving to build up treasures in heaven rather than treasures on earth (Matthew 6:19–21).
4. Giving to thank God for his blessings (Psalm 118:1).
5. Giving as a result of your love for God (2 Corinthians 8:7–8).

Our motives are important to God. As 1 Corinthians 4:5 says, "He will bring to light what is hidden in darkness and will expose the motives of the heart."

In summary, as you give to God's work, ensure that your motives are godly, and God will bless you abundantly.

11. Everyone Can Experience the Joy of Giving

You do not have to be wealthy to experience the joy of giving. In 2 Corinthians 8:1–4, Paul testified:

We want you to know about the grace that God has given the Macedonian churches. In the midst of a very severe trial, their overflowing joy and their extreme poverty welled up in rich generosity. For I testify that they gave as much as they were able, and even beyond their ability. Entirely on their own, they urgently pleaded with us for the privilege of sharing in this service to the Lord's people.

Notwithstanding their extreme poverty, the Macedonians gave generously and sacrificially out of their love for God. As a result, they experienced the joy of giving. As indicated in Galatians 5:22, one of the fruits of the Spirit is joy. The Macedonians experienced this through generous giving.

In summary, regardless of your income, you too can give generously and experience the joy of giving.

12. Give Cheerfully

God will bless those who give cheerfully and generously to his work. In 2 Corinthians 9:6–7, Paul said: "Whoever sows sparingly will also reap sparingly, and whoever sows generously will also reap generously. Each of you should give what you have decided in your heart to give, not reluctantly or under compulsion, for God loves a cheerful giver."

If you are not a cheerful giver, then I encourage you to prayerfully ask God to change your heart with respect to generosity. God can change anyone's heart, including the hearts of kings. "The king's heart is like channels of water in the hand of the LORD; He turns it wherever He pleases" (Proverbs 21:1, NASB).

Our hearts and motives are important to God. Proverbs 16:2 says, "All a person's ways seem pure to them, but motives are weighed by the LORD."

In summary, prayerfully ask God to enable you to give generously with a cheerful heart.

13. God Blesses Us so We Can Give Generously

In 2 Corinthians 9:10–11, Paul explained why God blesses us financially. "Now he who supplies seed to the sower and bread for food will also supply and increase your store of seed and will enlarge the harvest of your righteousness. You will be enriched in every way."

Why? So that you can spend what you receive on your own desires? No! Paul continued in verse 11, "So that you can be generous on every occasion, and through us your generosity will result in thanksgiving to God."

Here's the cycle. God blesses Christians so that we can give generously. In response, the Lord provides even more to the generous givers. Generous giving results in thanksgiving to God, meaning God is glorified through the generous giving of his servants.

In summary, God's purpose for blessing Christians is *not* to enable us to spend money as we wish. Rather, his purpose is for us to give generously so the Lord will be glorified!

14. When You Give to God's Work, Everyone Is Blessed

When you give to God's work, the blessings are at least threefold, as outlined here.

1. The people being ministered to are blessed because you have provided for their needs. In Matthew 10:42, Jesus said, "If anyone gives even a cup of cold water to one of these little ones who is my disciple, truly I tell you, that person will certainly not lose their reward."

2. When you give to God's work, those who carry out the ministry are blessed and encouraged by your giving. Here is Paul's response to the gifts he received from fellow believers: "I have received full payment and have more than enough. I am amply supplied, now that I have received from Epaphroditus the gifts you sent. They are a fragrant offering, an acceptable sacrifice, pleasing to God" (Philippians 4:18).

3. As you give to God's work, you, the giver, are also blessed. Jesus said, "It is more blessed to give than to receive" (Acts 20:35).

In summary, remember that everyone is blessed when you give to God's work!

15. Will a Man Rob God?

In Malachi 3:8–10, God said:

> "Will a mere mortal rob God? Yet you rob me. But you ask, 'How are we robbing you?'
>
> "In tithes and offerings. You are under a curse—your whole nation—because you are robbing me. Bring the whole tithe into the storehouse, that there may be food in my house. Test me in this," says the LORD Almighty, "and see if I will not throw open the floodgates of heaven and pour out so much blessing that there will not be room enough to store it."

Today, we are not under Mosaic Law. But Christ indirectly affirmed the principle of tithing in Matthew 23:23. So although we are not bound by legalism, the tithe is a guideline. Generally, it indicates the minimum amount most Christians should be giving to God's work.

In the New Testament, the emphasis is to give generously without specific percentages. For Christians with higher-than-average incomes, giving 10 per cent will be giving out of obedience, but not generous giving. For others, giving 10 per cent will be very sacrificial.

In summary, make it a priority to give the first 10 per cent of your income to God's work. God will bless your obedience!

16. Debt Hinders Giving

Over the past 44 years, I've seen the finances of thousands of people. I've noted that when Christians spend more than they earn and accumulate debt, their giving will decrease in order to pay their debts.

For example, assume an individual or couple has spent all of their regular income; they have a lot of debt and no savings. So, when they receive their paycheque and they have a big mortgage payment and car loan payment, and other debts coming due—what happens? They will pay their debts first and forgo giving to God's work. In my experience, the accumulation of debt is the most common hindrance to giving.

These Christians are experiencing the truth of Proverbs 22:7, that "the borrower is slave to the lender." Servicing their debts has taken priority over giving to God's work.

The long-term solution is to learn God's perspective on debt and how to get out of debt. Here are some initial steps.

1. Develop and implement a budget to ensure you spend less than you earn; use the surplus to pay down debt and give to God's work.
2. Study God's word on finances so you can avoid the many financial pitfalls that result from debt.
3. Learn to be content with less (Philippians 4:11–13).

To learn more about how to get out of debt, go through my workshop series titled "Debt Reduction God's Way," available at www.coplandfinancialministries.org.

17. Rob and Linda Give Less Because of Debt

In their first year of marriage, Rob and Linda faithfully gave 10 per cent of their income to the Lord's work. However, over several years, they did not track their expenses. They had no budget and unintentionally spent more than they earned, accumulating debt.

As their debts increased, their giving gradually decreased; eventually, they were giving less than 1 per cent of their income. They realized something was wrong, so they prayed and studied God's word on finances. Through Scripture, God revealed to Rob and Linda that they had unknowingly been violating several biblical financial principles.

Linda and Rob started recording their expenses. They reduced their lifestyle and implemented a budget to ensure they were spending less than they earned. Then they used the surplus to pay down debt and to give more to God's work. Within one year, they were tithing again and within three years they had paid off their credit cards and personal lines of credit. Now they experience God's peace in the area of finances and praise God for his wisdom in his word.

18. Give Generously Out of Your Love for God

God wants us to give generously out of our love and gratitude to him. In 2 Corinthians 8:7–8, Paul said, "Since you excel in everything—in faith, in speech, in knowledge, in complete earnestness and in the love we have kindled in you—see that you also excel in this grace of giving."

And in the next chapter, Paul continued by saying, "Whoever sows sparingly will also reap sparingly, and whoever sows generously will also reap generously. Each of you should give what you have decided in your heart to give, not reluctantly or under compulsion, for God loves a cheerful giver" (2 Corinthians 9:6–7).

God has blessed us abundantly; how can we not give generously back to God? As 2 Corinthians 9:11 says: "You will be enriched in every way so that you can be generous on every occasion, and through us your generosity will result in thanksgiving to God."

In summary, give generously and sacrificially to God's work out of your love, obedience, and trust in him.

19. Easy Credit Results in Reduced Giving

Offers of unsolicited credit cards, personal lines of credit, zero per cent financing, and retailer incentives—all of these things entice us to borrow money. Unfortunately, many Christians have yielded to these worldly temptations and accumulated debt. This generally leads them to reduce their giving because they are forced to make a choice between paying debts or giving to God's work.

Yet, as 1 Corinthians 10:13 says, "No temptation has over-taken you except what is common to mankind. And God is faith-ful; he will not let you be tempted beyond what you can bear. But when you are tempted, he will also provide a way out so that you can endure it."

In other words, Christians must avoid the temptation to bor-row and buy. For example, if you tend to overspend using credit cards, cut them up. Or if you tend to spend money buying tools you don't need, then purposely avoid the hardware store.

In summary, if you avoid the temptation of easy credit then you will be able to give more to God's work.

20. Minimal Debt Enables Generous Giving

Over the past 44 years, I've had the privilege of helping thousands of individuals and couples reduce their debt. Many of them become totally debt-free. One clear trend I've seen is that as a committed Christian's debt decreases, their giving generally increases.

The opposite is true as well. As a Christian's debt increases, their giving decreases almost without exception. Why? Because as debt increases, you become "a slave of the lender" (Proverbs 22:7). Your priority is to service your debts rather than giving to God's work.

Just imagine if you were debt-free. Think of the additional cash flow you would have each month—enabling you to give very generously to God's work! No wonder God's word clearly discourages debt.

In summary, with God's wisdom and direction, reduce your debt so you can increase your giving to God.

21. Christians Are Citizens of Heaven

As Christians, Paul said, "our citizenship is in heaven" (Philippians 3:20). Therefore heaven, not Earth, is our home. In light of our eternal citizenship in heaven, the wise Christian gives generously to God's work, rather than hoarding or using money for selfish purposes.

Always remember, money and material things in and of themselves are temporary. As Paul said, "We brought nothing into the world, and we can take nothing out of it" (1 Timothy 6:7).

However, a temporal asset such as money can be converted into an eternal asset by giving it to God's work. How significant are the rewards? In Matthew 19:29, God promised a hundred-fold return in heaven for those who give sacrificially to his work.

Therefore, as eternal citizens of heaven, it only makes sense to give generously to God's work. That's why Jesus said, "It is more blessed to give than to receive" (Acts 20:35).

22. What Constitutes Generous Giving?

What constitutes generous giving depends on each person's circumstances. For example, a high-income earner giving 10 per cent of their income is giving out of their surplus, but it is not generous giving. Meanwhile, for a low-income earner, giving 5 to 7 per cent of their income would likely represent sacrificial and generous giving.

In the parable of the widow (Luke 21), Christ explained that the widow gave more than the rich, even though the monetary value of her gift was very small. Why? Because her gift was sacrificial.

When was the last time you sacrificed in order to give to God's work? To the wealthy (which includes most of us) Jesus said, "From everyone who has been given much, much will be demanded" (Luke 12:48).

God is the one who will make the final judgment. Romans 14:12 says, "Each of us will give an account of ourselves to God."

In summary, make sure you are a generous giver.

23. Paul and Jill Give God the "Leftovers"

Over the past several years, Paul and Jill have incurred significant debt to acquire a large home, two nice cars, and new furniture. Even though they attend a Bible-believing church, they give sporadically to God's work—usually less than 2 per cent of their income.

When their pastor taught on giving, Jill and Paul discussed it and both concluded they would increase their giving after their debts were paid off. To justify this, they quote Romans 13:8, which says, "Let no debt remain outstanding."

Paul and Jill are giving God the leftovers, which is contrary to God's word. Proverbs 3:9 says, "Honor the LORD with your wealth, with the firstfruits of all your crops." Yes, they do have a responsibility to pay their off debts (Psalm 37:21), but they also have a responsibility to make giving to God's work a priority.

As Christians, we have a dual responsibility. We should pay our off debts and give to God's work simultaneously.

24. Be Faithful With a Small Amount
When Betty earned a below-average income several years ago, she didn't tithe because he believed she could not afford to. Today, Betty's income is significantly above average, but she still does not make giving to God's work a priority. Why? Jesus answers, "The one who is faithful in a very little thing is also faithful in much; and the one who is unrighteous in a very little thing is also unrighteous in much" (Luke 16:10, NASB).

Christ is saying, if you are not faithful to God with your current level of income, then you will not be faithful when you have more income. It's an issue of your priorities and commitment, not your level of income.

In the parable of the talents, the master (who represents God) entrusted more to the servants who were faithful in managing money God's way. But one of the servants was unfaithful, and the master took away what he had (Matthew 25:14–30).

In summary, make giving to God's work a priority at your current level of income. Don't wait any longer.

25. Parents' Money Management Impacts Their Children
For most of their life, Jim and Jane gave very little to God's work. Yet they owned many material things, like a nice home and new cars; they provided the latest and best of everything for their children. Now that they are grandparents, they finally realize that their worldly perspective on money has been adopted by their children.

Proverbs 22:6 says, "Start children off on the way they should go, and even when they are old they will not turn from it." Unfortunately, when parents manage money in a worldly fashion, that bad example will often be inherited by their children and their grandchildren. Although Jim and Jane are spiritually mature in other areas, they are spiritually immature in the financial area.

Hebrews 5:12 says, "Though by this time you ought to be teachers, you need someone to teach you the elementary truths of God's word all over again." Jim and Jane need to learn God's way of managing money. Then they should teach their children and grandchildren a biblical perspective on money and material things.

Go to www.coplandfinancialministries.org to learn more about God's word on finances. We have numerous resources there, most of which are free. You can also follow @biblefinance on Facebook, Instagram, and Twitter.

X.
FINANCIAL DECEPTIONS

1. Living Paycheque-to-Paycheque Is Foolish

A financial deception is a belief that appears to be correct but is contrary to God's word. This section includes several examples of financial deceptions and how you need to deal with them.

Today, most people live paycheque-to-paycheque; that is, they spend all their regular income and have no savings. For example, most people do not regularly save for non-monthly expenses, such as vacations or car repairs. In Proverbs 21:20, God says this is foolish; "The wise store up choice food and olive oil, but fools gulp theirs down." In his example of building a tower (Luke 14:28–30), Jesus communicated clearly that if you don't plan for future expenses, you are foolish.

So what should we do? Here's the biblical approach—set aside sufficient funds on a monthly basis to provide for non-monthly expenses. For example, if your annual vacation costs twelve hundred dollars, then you should save one hundred dollars per month throughout the year so you have sufficient funds to pay for it and avoid unnecessary debt.

In summary, living paycheque-to-paycheque is not consistent with God's word. God's admonition is that we should plan ahead and save for future needs.

2. Develop a Budget to Save for Future Needs

In the parable of the tower (Luke 14:28–30), Christ admonished us to plan ahead, which includes the need to save for future needs. In order to save for future needs, it's necessary to develop and implement a budget to ensure you regularly spend less than you earn so you have a monthly surplus.

Some future expenses, such as car and house repairs, car replacement, children's education, and retirement will have to be estimated. Nevertheless, it is generally possible to estimate and save for these future needs. Saving is biblical (Proverbs 21:20).

In summary, you need to develop and implement a budget to ensure you have sufficient savings for future needs.

How much do you need to save? Get Form 3 of the Copland budgeting system at www.coplandfinancialministries.org. It is a tool for estimating the monthly savings you need to meet future expenses .

3. Financial Freedom Doesn't Mean "Get Rich Quickly"

Many people believe the lie that it's good to try to get rich quickly. Some common methods used for this include purchasing lottery tickets, aggressive investing—usually with a lot of debt—and excessive hard work, which creates an out-of-balance life. So the deception from the world is to try to get rich quickly; God's directive is to plan and save for future needs relatively slowly and over a period of time.

Here are some key Scriptures: "Steady plodding brings prosperity; hasty speculation brings poverty" (Proverbs 21:5, TLB). In Proverbs 13:11, we read, "Dishonest money dwindles away, but whoever gathers money little by little makes it grow."

In summary, God's approach is to diligently plan ahead and save a little at a time over a long period of time, not to try to get rich quickly.

4. Don't Try to Get Rich Quickly: Earn Your Living Through Your Occupation

In 1 Timothy 6:9–11, Paul warned of the dangers of trying to get rich quickly:

> Those who want to get rich fall into temptation and a trap and into many foolish and harmful desires that plunge people into ruin and destruction. For the love of money is a root of all kinds of evil. Some people, eager for money, have wandered from the faith and pierced themselves with many griefs.

In other words, the love of money will detrimentally impact your faith and result in many problems. With respect to earning income, what then should we do? Proverbs 28:19–20 says, "Those who work their land will have abundant food, but those who chase fantasies will have their fill of poverty. A faithful person will be richly blessed, but one eager to get rich will not go unpunished."

Given that most people were farmers at the time this passage was written, God is saying you should focus on earning a reasonable income from your occupation, not trying to get rich quickly.

5. Debt Restructuring Treats the Symptom, Not the Problem

Over the past 44 years, I have counselled thousands of people who have accumulated significant credit card debt. Generally, someone will advise them to obtain a line of credit to pay off their expensive credit card debts. At this point, many people believe this has solved their financial problems.

However, since their bad financial habits continue, generally within about three years they have maxed out their credit cards and must obtain additional financing—perhaps a second mortgage on their home. If they continue to manage money in the same manner, within a few years, they will be forced to draw money from their retirement account.

All along, people in this situation believe the lie that debt restructuring will solve their financial problems. In reality, it only treats a symptom. The real problem is that they are spending more than they earn. They must implement a budget to ensure they spend less than they earn and use the monthly surplus to pay down their debts.

6. Financial Problems Often Reflect Spiritual Problems

People in financial difficulty often seek solutions through earning more income or debt restructuring. But sometimes the root cause of the problem is spiritual in nature, not financial. For example, the attitudes of covetousness, greed, selfishness, and pride reflect spiritual immaturity and are contrary to God's word.

Christians who struggle with these worldly mindsets must change the way they think about money. Romans 12:2 says, "Do not conform to the pattern of this world, but be transformed by the renewing of your mind. Then you will be able to test and approve what God's will is—his good, pleasing and perfect will."

Permanent change only occurs in those Christians who habitually study God's word on finances. Why? Because as Paul said, "All Scripture is God-breathed and is useful for teaching, rebuking, correcting and training in righteousness, so that the servant of God may be thoroughly equipped for every good work" (2 Timothy 3:16–17).

In summary, regularly study what the Bible says about finances in order to develop a godly mindset with respect to money and material things.

7. Money Doesn't Guarantee Happiness

Many people believe the deception that money brings happiness. Although additional income can help, money in and of itself doesn't bring happiness. Since 1982, I've advised thousands of people with significant wealth who aren't happy. They aren't experiencing God's peace. Instead, they are worried, wondering, *What if I lose my money?* Or *Where shall I invest my money?*

In Ecclesiastes 5:10, God warned, "Whoever loves money never has money enough; whoever loves wealth is never satisfied with their income." In other words, money and material things will never truly satisfy.

The only way to be happy and experience "the peace of God, which transcends all understanding" (Philippians 4:7) is through a close relationship with Jesus and through managing money God's way. In John 14:27, Jesus said, "Peace I leave with you; my peace I give you. I do not give to you as the world gives."

In summary, if you are not experiencing God's peace, I encourage you to develop a close personal relationship with the Lord Jesus Christ and manage money according to biblical principles.

8. God's Peace Comes from a Relationship With Christ

Over the last 40 years, I've seen many people who have significant income and lots of material things, yet they are frustrated, angry, weary, and unhappy. If you feel this way, consider Christ's invitation in Matthew 11:28–30, "Come to me, all you who are weary and burdened, and I will give you rest. Take my yoke upon you and learn from me, for I am gentle and humble in heart, and you will find rest for your souls. For my yoke is easy and my burden is light."

Christ wants us to yoke with him—that is, to develop a close personal relationship with the Lord. In John 15, Jesus called this abiding, which means being connected to and in communication with God continuously. As you develop your relationship with Christ, you will experience the fruits of the Spirit, including God's peace and joy (Galatians 5:22–23).

God's peace and joy do not come from having more money. They can only be experienced through a close personal relationship with the Lord Jesus Christ.

9. Buying Now, Paying Later Doesn't Pay Off

Today, easy credit creates many temptations to buy now and pay later. Consequently, many people buy things on credit they cannot afford. God's directive is different. He wants us to prayerfully ask him to meet our needs and then wait for his provision. "The LORD is my portion; therefore I will wait for him" (Lamentations 3:24).

I've seen many situations where God met needs in unusual ways. For example, one Christian couple with a modest income needed to replace their car. They prayerfully asked God to provide and waited for his provision. Within a few months, a fellow believer gave them a used car in excellent shape. They realized that if they had not prayed and waited upon the Lord, they would have missed God's blessing.

So when you have a need, I encourage you to pray and wait upon the Lord. God can provide in many ways, such as unexpected income, a better deal, a gift, or another alternative.

10. Put God First and God Will Provide

Most people buy things on credit without consulting God and without waiting for his provision. In Matthew 6:31–33, Christ promised to meet our needs if we put him first. Here's what he said:

> "Do not worry, saying, 'What shall we eat? or 'What shall we drink?' or 'What shall we wear?' For the pagans run after all these things, and your heavenly Father knows that you need them. But seek first his kingdom and his righteousness, and all these things will be given to you as well."

Note that God promises to meet our *needs* but not necessarily our *wants and desires*. In addition, God instructs us to be content: Hebrews 13:5 says, "Keep your lives free from the love of money and be content with what you have, because God has said, 'Never will I leave you; never will I forsake you.'"

In summary, put God first, trust him to meet your needs, and be content with his provision and timing. God will provide.

11. Smart People Use Little or No Debt, Not Other People's Money

Many people believe the deception that smart people use other people's money, not their own. This is true only if you could predict the direction of the markets so that you could profit from borrowed money. However, in Proverbs 27:1, God warned, "Do not boast about tomorrow, for you do not know what a day may bring."

History demonstrates the truth of this proverb. For example, from 2002 until June of 2008, the value of most stocks on the Toronto and New York stock exchanges increased significantly. With false confidence, many people borrowed money to increase their returns.

However, from June 2008 until March 2009, most stocks decreased by about 50 per cent. Those who used debt incurred huge losses. Similarly, in March 2020 during the COVID-19 pandemic, the general stock market decreased about 32 per cent. Again, those who use debt aggressively were forced to sell at the wrong time, when the market was way down.

Further, many businesses try to use debt to their advantage. Unfortunately, almost every business will encounter difficult times, and those with the most debt suffer the most.

Smart people do not use other people's money; rather, they borrow as little as possible and pay down their debts as soon as possible.

12. Only God Knows the Future, Therefore Follow God's Will

Another common deception is that smart people can figure out the future direction of the markets and make lots of money. This is not true. Historically, on average, only about 15 per cent of all professional money managers beat the relevant indices; no one can consistently predict the direction of the markets. The market crashes in 2008 and 2020 demonstrate that no human knows the future.

Whether you are investing or operating a business, heed God's warning in James 4:13–15:

> Now listen, you who say, "Today or tomorrow we will go to this or that city, spend a year there, carry on business and make money." Why, you do not even know what will happen tomorrow. What is your life? You are a mist that appears for a little while and then vanishes. Instead, you ought to say, "If it is the Lord's will, we will live and do this or that."

In other words, there are no sure deals. In summary, since we don't know the future, we need to ensure that every major financial decision is the Lord's will through praying and studying God's word.

13. Contentment Leads to God's True Financial Freedom

Most people believe that financial freedom is obtained by having lots of money. This is a deception! In my experience, most people who have lots of money are worried, frustrated, and unhappy. The reason why is because true financial freedom comes from experiencing God's peace about your finances.

One key element for achieving God's peace is contentment. In 1 Timothy 6:6–8, Paul said, "Godliness with contentment is great gain. For we brought nothing into the world, and we can take nothing out of it. But if we have food and clothing, we will be content with that."

Contentment does not come automatically; it has to be learned. In Philippians 4:11–13, Paul said:

> I have learned to be content whatever the circumstances. I know what it is to be in need, and I know what it is to have plenty. I have learned the secret of being content in any and every situation, whether well fed or hungry, whether living in plenty or in want. I can do all this through him who gives me strength.

And remember, Paul wrote this when he was in prison. We can see he was able to learn contentment because of his close relationship with Jesus Christ and his focus on things of eternal value.

Learn to be content with God's provision. Then you will experience the Lord's peace and true financial freedom.

14. Financial Security Doesn't Result in Financial Freedom

One of the deceptions of this world is that financial freedom comes from having lots of money and financial security. But, like the rich fool in Luke 12, many people never feel that they have acquired enough. Why? Ecclesiastes 5:10 answers, "Whoever loves money never has enough; whoever loves wealth is never satisfied with their income."

In order to experience God's true financial freedom, you need to learn his truths regarding money and be freed from the deceptions of this world. In John 8:31–32, Jesus said, "If you hold to my teaching, you are really my disciples. Then you will know the truth, and the truth will set you free."

Also, give generously. Jesus said, "It is more blessed to give than to receive" (Acts 20:35). Giving with a cheerful heart and out of your love for God enables you to be free from the love of money and to experience the joy of giving. Trusting in God's truth and following his financial principles will enable you to experience the Lord's true financial freedom.

15. Stewards Should Build Up Treasures in Heaven

Holding too tightly to materials things will produce financial stress rather than financial freedom. In Psalm 50:9–12, God said:

> "I have no need of a bull from your stall or of goats from your pens, for every animal of the forest is mine, and the cattle on a thousand hills. I know every bird in the mountains, and the insects in the fields are mine. If I were hungry I would not tell you, for the world is mine, and all that is in it."

Remember, most people were farmers during Old Testament times. In other words, God is saying he owns everything; our financial resources are a temporary loan from him.

Hence, we are stewards of what God has entrusted to us. Our responsibility is to apply his financial principles and do his will. In Matthew 6:31–33, Jesus promised that if we put him first, he will meet our needs. Once you have fulfilled your responsibilities, you can "cast your cares on the LORD and he will sustain you; he will never let the righteous be shaken" (Psalm 55:22). Therefore, you can trust God to meet your needs, and this should enable you to enjoy the Lord's peace.

Remember, money and material things are temporary and not of any eternal value. That's why Jesus instructed us in Matthew 6:19–21 to build up treasures in heaven, rather than treasures on earth.

16. Bankruptcy Treats the Symptom, Not the Problem

Many people believe the deception that declaring bankruptcy will solve their financial problems. But numerous statistics—and many cases I have seen—reveal that the majority who go bankrupt get into financial trouble again, with many declaring bankruptcy a second time. Why? Because bankruptcy treats the symptom (excessive debt), not the problem.

Almost always, the real problem is the violation of God's financial principles. These violations generally continue after an individual goes bankrupt. It is not God's will for a Christian to declare bankruptcy. Besides being a bad testimony (Matthew 5:14–16), as Psalm 37:21 says, "The wicked borrow and do not repay." In other words, it is a sin to borrow money and not repay it.

Since 1982, I have counselled thousands of people in financial difficulty. The Lord blessed in unusual ways those who learned and implemented God's financial principles. Almost all of them avoided bankruptcy. If you are in financial difficulty, you must learn and implement God's financial principles—this is the best long-term solution.

17. You Can Recover from Bankruptcy

Psalm 37:21 is clear that Christians should not declare bankruptcy. It is a sin and a bad testimony (Matthew 5:14–16). However, if you have declared bankruptcy already, allow me to encourage you in several ways.

1. God loves you and will forgive you (1 John 1:9) if you confess your act of bankruptcy and other sins that may have contributed to going bankrupt—such as covetousness, selfishness, greed, or lack of contentment.
2. Develop and implement a budget to ensure you spend less than you earn and have a surplus to pay down debts and save for future needs.
3. Study God's word on finances, and prayerfully ask the Lord to reveal the real causes of your bankruptcy. Most Christians unknowingly violate God's financial principles and struggle with ungodly attitudes such as covetousness, selfishness, greed, or lack of contentment.

Generally, it's the violation of biblical principles and ungodly attitudes that cause people to get into debt and eventually go bankrupt. Living by God's financial principles will enable you to recover from bankruptcy and avoid the debt trap again.

18. The Deceitfulness of Wealth

Wealth can be deceitful and hinder our spiritual growth. Jesus said, "The seed falling among the thorns refers to someone who hears the word, but the worries of this life and the deceitfulness of wealth choke the word, making it unfruitful" (Matthew 13:22).

How is wealth deceitful? As we accumulate money and material things, it's very easy to trust in these temporary assets, rather than in God. For example, after being blessed with a large crop, the rich fool in Luke 12 decided to hoard his wealth rather than share it. He trusted in his wealth rather than trusting in God.

Yes, we need some money to buy necessities. And God has promised to provide these things if we put him first (Matthew 6:31–33). However, we must never put our trust in money or material things.

God admonished us, "Trust in the LORD with all your heart, and lean not on your own understanding; in all your ways acknowledge Him, and He shall direct your paths" (Proverbs 3:5–6, NKJV).

19. The Pursuit of Wealth

In this world, it is very tempting to pursue wealth since most people believe it will solve all their problems. Yet in Proverbs 23:4–5, God instructed us, "Do not wear yourself out to get rich; do not trust your own cleverness. Cast but a glance at riches, and they are gone, for they will surely sprout wings and fly off to the sky like an eagle."

In Matthew 6:19–21, Jesus warned that money and material things are temporary. Therefore, we should invest in things of eternal value.

"Do not store up for yourselves treasures on earth, where moths and vermin destroy, and where thieves break in and steal. But store up for yourselves treasures in heaven, where moths and vermin do not destroy, and where thieves do not break in and steal. For where your treasure is, there your heart will be also."

For clarification, there is nothing wrong with having wealth. God entrusted wealth to many faithful servants, such as Abraham, Solomon, and Job. Rather, it is the selfish pursuit of wealth that is contrary to God's will.

So I encourage you to prayerfully ask God to reveal your motives for pursuing money and material things. Are your motives godly or worldly? Proverbs 16:2 states, "All a person's ways seem pure to them, but motives are weighed by the LORD."

20. Spend Less Than You Earn and Save for Future Needs

Over the past 40 years, Rod and Sue both earned above-average incomes. They want to retire, so they assessed their financial position. They were disappointed to realize that they couldn't retire for at least 15 years because they had to pay off their debts and save more for retirement.

In light of their debts, Rod and Sue probably believed it was okay to buy now and pay later. They now realize the truth of Proverbs 22:7. They had become "a slave to the lender" because they must work full-time in order to service their debts, notwithstanding their health problems.

Unfortunately, Rod and Sue believed the financial deception that it is okay to live paycheque-to-paycheque; they spent most of their income and didn't save for future needs. This is contrary to Scripture. "The wise man saves for the future, but the foolish man spends whatever he gets" (Proverbs 21:20, TLB).

In summary, diligently spend less than you earn and save for future needs.

21. Managing Money God's Way Results in God's Blessings: Real-Life Example

During his twenties, Rick planned to become wealthy by using debt to increase his investment returns. In other words, Rick believed the financial deception that smart people use other people's money. Unfortunately, Rick's investments decreased significantly in value. Because of his debts, he lost his original capital, resulting in a large deficit. As a result, Rick had to work additional hours in order to service his debts.

During his thirties, Rick learned God's key financial principles. He realized he was a steward of what God had entrusted to him and that he should use minimal debt or no debt. Rick learned contentment and he experienced the joy of giving. Proverbs 28:20 says, "A faithful person will be richly blessed."

As a result of Rick's faithful stewardship, God blessed Rick with an excellent job and reasonable investment returns. In the long run, managing money God's way provides financial stability, contentment, and God's blessings. Psalm 128:1 says, "Blessed are all who fear the LORD, who walk in obedience to him."

Go to www.coplandfinancialministries.org to learn more about God's word on finances. We have numerous resources there, most of which are free. You can also follow @biblefinance on Facebook, Instagram, and Twitter.

XI.
CO-SIGNING

1. The Bible Warns Against Co-Signing

Most Christians aren't aware that God's word strongly advises against co-signing for other people's loans. "It's a dangerous thing to guarantee payment for someone's debts. Don't do it!" (Proverbs 11:15, CEV).

Several chapters later, Proverbs again states, "Don't guarantee to pay someone else's debt. If you don't have the money, you might lose your bed" (Proverbs 22:26–27, CEV). God warned that if you co-sign on someone else's loan, you might lose your bed, which means you could lose something valuable to you, such as your home, your car, or your retirement fund.

Since 1982, I have seen hundreds of cases where an individual has co-signed on someone else's loan. Often, the borrower defaults, and the co-signer is forced to pay the debt. Most people don't understand this risk when they co-sign. God's word regarding co-signing is a principle, not a law. It is not a sin to co-sign, but God clearly warned of the dangers of doing so.

2. Co-Signing Can Ruin Relationships

Several years ago, I received a phone call from a distressed woman who explained that the bank had just taken a significant portion of her and her husband's retirement funds to pay for their adult son's loan.

Without understanding the risks or the biblical principle admonishing us not to co-sign (Proverbs 11:15; Proverbs 22:26–27) these parents had co-signed on a loan for their adult son and daughter-in-law. After the young couple had missed several payments, the bank legally demanded the loan and unilaterally used the co-signer's money to pay it off.

As well as losing a lot of money, this couple lost the good relationship they had with their son and daughter-in-law. The younger couple felt guilty because of what happened. Invitations for dinner were turned down, and both parties found it awkward when they got together.

The parent's motives for co-signing were fine. They did so out of love, but they had no idea that most of the time, co-signers have to pay the borrower's debt and it will often sour the relationship.

3. It's Better to Give Than to Co-Sign

God discourages co-signing for a loan. "It's poor judgment to guarantee another person's debt or put up security for a friend" (Proverbs 17:18, NLT). Most of the time, the co-signer ends up having to pay the debt. This is no surprise since the lender requires a co-signer because they believe the borrower is not credit-worthy.

I personally never co-sign for anyone. If a friend or relative has a real need, I will pray, and—if directed by the Lord—I will give them the money. Another option, if you are led by the Lord, is to lend your own money with Jesus's mindset of lending without expecting anything in return (Luke 6:38). If you give or lend the funds expecting nothing in return, then even if the borrower defaults on the loan you won't be subject to legal action from a bank, and your relationship with the borrower should remain intact.

In summary, don't co-sign. If God directs you—and assuming you can afford to—consider giving or lending your own money.

4. Free Yourself from a Co-Signed Loan

Statistics demonstrate that when someone co-signs for a loan, more than 50 per cent of the time it is the co-signer, not the borrower, who ends up paying the loan. We should not be surprised by this since generally a bank only requires a co-signer when the borrower is a high credit risk.

If you have already co-signed for a loan, God instructs you to do everything possible to free yourself from that responsibility. Proverbs 6:1–5 states:

> My son, if you have put up security for your neighbor, if you have shaken hands in pledge for a stranger, you have been trapped by what you said, ensnared by the words of your mouth. So do this, my son, to free yourself, since you have fallen into your neighbor's hands: Go—to the point of exhaustion—and give your neighbor no rest! Allow no sleep to your eyes, no slumber to your eyelids. Free yourself, like a gazelle from the hand of the hunter, like a bird from the snare of the fowler.

If you have co-signed a loan, prayerfully ask God to provide a way to free yourself from the obligation.

5. Ways to Get Free of Co-Signed Obligations

The Bible advises against co-signing for a loan, but if you have already done so, here are some suggestions to free yourself from that obligation. First, prayerfully ask God for his wisdom (James 1:5) and direction (Psalm 32:8) on how to free yourself from the co-signing obligation.

Next, ask the lender if he is willing to eliminate your co-signing obligation. Often, God has to provide a mini miracle for this to happen, because rarely will the lender release the co-signer. Nevertheless, we know that the heart of anyone (including a lender) is in God's hands. "The king's heart is a stream of water in the hand of the LORD; he turns it wherever he will" (Proverbs 21:1, ESV).

You could also try to find another financial institution to lend the borrower money without a co-signer, and then use those funds to pay off the loan that you co-signed. Most importantly, teach the borrower God's way of managing money to reduce the risk of a default.

In summary, with God's wisdom and direction, free yourself from any co-signing obligations.

6. The Dangers of Providing Personal Guarantees for Corporate Debt

Often, business owners give personal guarantees for their company's debt. Proverbs 11:15 warns against this. "Whoever puts up security for a stranger will surely suffer, but whoever refuses to shake hands in pledge is safe."

When the Book of Proverbs was written, business deals were confirmed with a handshake. To "strike hands in pledge" meant to shake hands confirming a pledge to pay a financial obligation. When a business owner provides a personal guarantee, they are pledging personal assets for company debt. God warned against this.

Proverbs 22:26–27 states, "Do not be one who shakes hands in pledge or puts up security for debts; if you lack the means to pay, your very bed will be snatched from under you." In other words, if your company cannot pay the debt, your very bed, or perhaps your home, could be taken from you.

Avoiding personal guarantees is a biblical principle, not a law. It is not a sin to guarantee your company's debt, but God clearly discourages giving personal guarantees for corporate debt.

7. Avoid Co-Signing for Corporate Debts

When a business owner gives a personal guarantee for their company's debt, the individual is assuming that the company's profits will be sufficient to service the debt. In other words, they are presuming on the future. James 4:13–15 warns against this:

> Now listen, you who say, "Today or tomorrow we will go to this or that city, spend a year there, carry on business and make money." Why, you do not even know what will happen tomorrow. What is your life? You are a mist that appears for a little while and then vanishes. Instead, you ought to say, "If it is the Lord's will, we will live and do this or that."

Further, this warning in Proverbs says, "It's a dangerous thing to guarantee payment for someone's debts. Don't do it!" (Proverbs 11:15, CEV). In other words, it is God's will that business owners avoid giving personal guarantees for corporate debt.

By refusing to give a personal guarantee, you protect your family's assets. In addition, if your business encounters financial difficulties you are in a much better negotiating position with your bank. Proverbs 14:15 states, "The prudent give thought to their steps."

In summary, it is biblical to avoid providing personal guarantees for your company's debts. And if you ever absolutely have to provide a personal guarantee for corporate debt, then set a maximum on that guarantee—for example, perhaps 50 per cent of what your company is borrowing. This reduces your risk and limits the negative personal consequences if your company should ever go bankrupt.

8. Free Yourself from Personal Guarantees

As indicated in Proverbs 22:26–27, it is biblical to avoid giving personal guarantees for your company's debts. However, if you have already given your personal guarantee, then Proverbs 6:1–3 admonishes you to free yourself. Here are some practical suggestions.

Develop and implement corporate and a personal budget (Luke 14:28–30) to ensure you spend less than you earn so you have a surplus to pay down debt. Once you have paid down the debt to an acceptable level, ask the bank to forgo your personal guarantees. You can also obtain equity investors in order to reduce your corporate debt. Or find a bank that will provide the same corporate financing with no personal guarantees and then switch banks.

Another option is to sell some assets of the business to lower the debt. God's best plan is to have no debt. However, if your company must borrow some money, then do it with no personal guarantees.

Depend upon God to enable you to eliminate your personal guarantees for corporate debt.

Go to www.coplandfinancialministries.org to learn more about God's word on finances. We have numerous resources there, most of which are free. You can also follow @biblefinance on Facebook, Instagram, and Twitter.

XII.
MANAGING MONEY DURING DIFFICULT TIMES, INCLUDING A PANDEMIC

1. God Is in Control Regardless of Difficult Circumstances
Are you worried about the impact events such as a health crisis or a market crash can have on your finances? Have you lost your job, or are you fearful that you could lose your job?

For example, a worldwide crisis like the COVID-19 pandemic triggered incredible fear throughout the world. But the God who created the heavens and the earth (Genesis 1) is still in control. Psalm 103:19 says, "The LORD has established his throne in heaven, and his kingdom rules over all."

In 1 Chronicles 29:11–12, after the building of the temple, David praised God with these words:

> "Yours, LORD, is the greatness and the power and the glory and the majesty and the splendor, for everything in heaven and earth is yours. Yours, LORD, is the kingdom; you are exalted as head over all. Wealth and honor come from you; you are the ruler of all things. In your hands are strength and power to exalt and give strength to all."

I do not believe God causes crises like pandemics, but that he allows them—very likely as a wake-up call to this world so that people will turn to him.

2. Experiencing God's Peace During a Crisis
It is possible to experience God's peace in the midst of severe trials. How? Develop a close personal relationship with the Lord Jesus Christ and focus on his word; pray fervently to the Lord

to provide for your needs (Philippians 4:19) and to give you his peace, regardless of your circumstances.

In John 14:27, Jesus said, "Peace I leave with you; my peace I give you. I do not give as the world gives. Do not let your hearts be troubled and do not be afraid." In John 16:32, Jesus explained to his disciples that a time was coming when they would face very severe trials—difficulties like most people are experiencing today. But Jesus said, "I have told you these things, so that in me you may have peace. In this world you will have trouble. But take heart! I have overcome the world" (John 16:33).

When people are fearful and anxious about their finances, they will often make hasty decisions. Proverbs 19:2 warns that hasty decisions are usually bad decisions. Experiencing God's peace—regardless of your financial problems—is good for your own health and well-being. It will also enable you to think in a clear, logical, and biblical fashion when dealing with your finances.

The first step to obtaining God's peace is prayer. Philippians 4:4–7 says:

> Rejoice in the Lord always. I will say it again: Rejoice! Let your gentleness be evident to all. The Lord is near. Do not be anxious about anything, but in every situation, by prayer and petition, with thanksgiving, present your requests to God. And the peace of God, which transcends all understanding, will guard your hearts and your minds in Christ Jesus.

As you pray and draw close to the Lord, God will give you his peace. "Now may the Lord of peace Himself continually grant you peace in every circumstance" (2 Thessalonians 3:16, NASB).

To learn more about how to experience God's peace during financial difficulties, go to www.coplandfinancialministries.org and watch the Financial Moments series titled "Peace and Anxiety."

3. God Promises to Meet Our Needs If We Put Him First

Regardless of what is happening with the economy or whatever crisis you face, God has promised to meet your needs if you put him first. In Matthew 6:31–33, Jesus said:

> "Do not worry, saying, 'What shall we eat? or 'What shall we drink?' or 'What shall we wear?' For the pagans run after all these things, and your heavenly Father knows that you need them. But seek first his kingdom and his righteousness, and all these things will be given to you as well."

In order to put God first, you need to manage money according to his principles and specific will. As you do that, God has promised to meet your needs, but not necessarily your wants and desires.

I would encourage you to review your credit card and bank statements for the past couple of years. Identify those expenditures that were wants and desires as opposed to needs. Often, a lot of money is spent unnecessarily on wants and desires, resulting in significant debt. If you've accumulated debt, then you need to eliminate those unnecessary expenses going forward.

In summary, put God first by managing money his way and the Lord will meet your needs.

4. Add Up Your Debts and Determine Where Your Money Is Going

Even if it is discouraging, list out all of your debts. It is best to understand your financial facts because making guesses about your debts—and your finances in general—is dangerous. Proverbs 27:23 says, "Be sure you know the condition of your flocks, give careful attention to your herds."

At the time this proverb was written, most people were farmers. The practical application of this biblical principle today is to know where you're at financially. This includes understanding exactly what your debts are, knowing your interest rates and repayment schedules, and determining where your money has been spent.

Proverbs 24:3–4 states, "By wisdom a house is built, and through understanding it is established; through knowledge its rooms are filled with rare and beautiful treasures." You need to have God's wisdom, understanding, and knowledge in order to manage money wisely.

In order to track your expenses, list your debts, and develop a budget, go to www.coplandfinancialministries.org. There, you can download a free copy of the Copland budgeting system and watch the free half-hour instructional video.

5. Develop and Implement a Budget

In the parable of the tower (Luke 14:28–30), Christ admonished us to plan ahead. The most practical way to do this is to develop and implement a budget or spending plan to ensure that you at least have a balanced budget each month—or even better, a surplus—in order to pay down debt and save for future needs.

To do this, you will likely have to eliminate all or almost all discretionary expenses. You may also need to increase your income where possible, such as through additional jobs or obtaining government assistance. If you still have a deficit in your budget, consider selling some assets, such as one of your cars. If absolutely necessary, downsize your home in order to pay down debt and provide funds needed for necessary expenditures.

Of interest, only a very small percentage of people manage their monthly cash flow well. However, if they learn and follow the biblical guidelines, including tracking their expenses and following a budget, then they will be much better off long-term.

In summary, managing your monthly cash flow according to biblical principles is critical to getting your finances in order.

6. Study and Meditate Upon God's Word Regularly

Most people violate biblical financial principles unknowingly and later suffer the consequences. I've been teaching God's word on finances since 1982, and I can say with conviction that those who follow biblical financial principles are better off in the long run. When tough times arise, such as a job loss or a severe recession, they will have minimal or no debt and significant savings. This will enable them to endure unexpected challenges far easier than most.

In Genesis 41, God revealed to Joseph that there would be seven years of plenty and seven years of famine. During the seven years of plenty, God instructed that the Egyptians should save for the tough times. Most people don't save during the good times, but rather accumulate significant debt and have no savings.

Most individuals, including government leaders, are not aware of the financial wisdom in the Bible. As a result, we now face incredible instability and uncertainty in our economy. The solution is to study and implement what the Bible says about finances.

7. The Joseph Principle

Some people refer to the "Joseph Principle." This is a biblical principle that should be followed by everyone—including individuals, corporations, and governments. In Genesis 41,

God enabled Joseph to interpret Pharaoh's dream. The Lord warned Joseph that there would be seven years of plenty and seven years of famine. God instructed Joseph to help the people prepare by saving 20 per cent of their grain during the seven years of plenty so they would have sufficient food during the seven years of famine.

In James 4:13–16, we are warned not to presume on the future, which most people do by spending all of their income and not saving for future needs. Yet most people will experience a "famine" of some kind at some point in their lives, such as a job loss or illness, that results in the loss of income.

Save money on a regular basis so you have a cushion of cash (Proverbs 21:20) to fall back on when you encounter difficult times. Generally, I recommend that individuals and couples have savings to cover at least six to nine months of expenses for unforeseen expenditures or loss of income.

8. God Has a Plan and a Purpose in Any Trial He Allows in Your Life

For those who believe in God, Jeremiah 29:11 states, "'For I know the plans I have for you,' declares the LORD, 'plans to prosper you and not to harm you, plans to give you hope and a future.'"

If you're out of work and encountering significant financial problems, you may wonder, *Where is God's great plan in all of this*? Remember, God is in control (Psalm 103:19) and will often allow trials in our lives (John 15:2) to teach us something. Perhaps the Lord may want us to learn more about biblical money management, or he could be using trials to draw us into closer relationships with him.

Romans 8:28 says, "We know that in all things God works for the good of those who love him, who have been called according to his purpose." I've experienced many trials in my life. When the trials come, I prayerfully ask God what he wants me to learn so he can bless me more here on earth and especially in eternity in heaven.

For the Christian who perseveres under trial, 1 Peter 1:6–7 says:

> In all this you greatly rejoice, though now for a little while you may have had to suffer grief in all kinds of trials. These have come so that the proven genuineness of your faith—of greater worth than gold, which perishes even though refined by fire—may result in praise, glory and honor when Jesus Christ is revealed.

In summary, when you encounter any financial difficulties, ask God what you need to learn or what you should do differently in the future. Positively embrace the trial with the objective of developing a closer relationship with the Lord (John 15:5).

9. Regardless of the Difficulty, There Is Hope for Your Financial Mess

Regardless of how difficult your financial problems are, God, with his "incomparably great power" (Ephesians 1:19) is able to solve any financial mess. If you're in financial difficulty, I recommend the following:

1. Pray and ask God for his wisdom and specific direction. In Isaiah 48:17, God promised, "I am the LORD your God, who teaches you what is best for you, who directs you in the way you should go."
2. Meditate on God's word. With over 2,300 references in the Bible that deal with money, God's word contains in-

credible wisdom on finances. And generally, the Bible's wisdom contradicts the world's wisdom.

3. Develop and follow a budget to ensure you're spending less than you earn and use the surplus to pay down debt and save for future needs. "The plans of the diligent certainly lead to advantage" (Proverbs 21:5, NASB).

I've provided biblical counsel to thousands of people since 1982, and I can say with conviction that our God can help you get out of any financial mess. He is the King of kings and the Lord of lords, the God of the universe. The Lord created the earth in six days, so he can help you solve your financial problems. Remember, "all things are possible with God" (Mark 10:27).

10. A Call to Prayer for Christians

As I wrote this, the world was still battling the COVID-19 pandemic. The Lord directed me to 2 Chronicles 7:14 in a powerful way. The verse says, "If my people, who are called by my name, will humble themselves and pray and seek my face and turn from their wicked ways, then I will hear from heaven, and I will forgive their sin and will heal their land."

I strongly believe that if Christians unite to pray for a spiritual revival throughout the world, we will see God heal us. Further, be sure to learn and apply God's financial principles and discern his specific will in managing the money that he has entrusted to you.

In the process, remember, "God has not given us a spirit of fear, but of power and of love and of a sound mind" (2 Timothy 1:7, NKJV). Do not fear. Rather, focus on the Lord and trust him (Proverbs 3:5–6) to direct you and meet your needs as you put him first (Matthew 6:31–33).

11. A Message for Non-Believers: How to Accept Christ as Saviour and Lord

If you do not have a personal relationship with Jesus Christ, I encourage you to consider these truths. God loves you and wants a personal relationship with you (John 10:14–18).

However, our sins have separated us from God. Romans 3:23 says that "all have sinned and fall short of the glory of God." God sent his only son, Jesus Christ, to die on the cross and pay the penalty for our sins. Romans 5:8 says, "God demonstrates his own love for us in this: While we were still sinners, Christ died for us."

In your heart, pray the following prayer:

Dear God,

I know I am a sinner and that I need your forgiveness.

I believe Jesus Christ died for my sins.

I am willing to turn from my sins.

I now invite you to come into my heart and life as my personal saviour.

I am willing, by God's strength, to follow and obey Jesus Christ as the Lord of my life.

In Jesus's name, amen.

If you prayed that prayer for the first time, I encourage you to send me an email to tcopland@zing-net.ca. I'd love to provide you with some additional information.

12. God Has a Purpose in Trials

Psalm 139 tells us that God is aware of every detail of our lives—including the financial problems that we face due to unforeseen crises. Although God does not cause our financial problems, he allows them to occur. God has a purpose for any trial his children encounter. Perhaps you have unknowingly violated some of his financial principles, in which case God's purpose may be to teach you something.

Or perhaps your financial problems are God's way of pruning you so you will bear more spiritual fruit, as Jesus talked about in John 15:2. Either way, God is still in control. In Isaiah 46:10–11, God said: "'My purpose will stand, and I will do all that I please.' From the east I summon a bird of prey; from a far-off land, a man to fulfill my purpose. What I have said, that I will bring about; what I have planned, that I will do."

Because God is in control, we need to trust him and depend solely on him for the direction and strength we need to deal with financial problems.

13. Financial Problems Can Be God Pruning Us

In John 15:1–2, Jesus said, "I am the true vine, and my Father is the gardener. He cuts off every branch in me that bears no fruit, while every branch that does bear fruit he prunes so that it will be even more fruitful."

Often, God will prune us by allowing trials in our life in order to draw us into a closer relationship with the Lord. Why is it so important to have a close relationship with the Lord? Jesus answers in John 15:4–5:

> Remain in me, as I also remain in you. No branch can bear fruit by itself; it must remain in the vine. Neither can you bear fruit unless you remain in me. I am the vine; you are the branches. If you remain in me and I in you, you will bear much fruit; apart from me you can do nothing.

Christ is saying we cannot bear spiritual fruit that will last for eternity unless we remain in a close personal relationship with him.

14. Don't Miss the Opportunity to Grow Closer to the Lord

Crises cause great fear and uncertainty. For example, when COVID-19 became a global crisis in early 2020, many people lived in great fear and worried about the future. Some people lost their jobs, some lost their homes, and many people suffered financially.

James 1:2–4 says:

> Consider it pure joy, my brothers and sisters, whenever you face trials of many kinds, because you know that the testing of your faith produces perseverance. Let perseverance finish its work so that you may be mature and complete, not lacking anything.

In other words, it's through trials that our faith is tested and we develop perseverance, enabling us to become spiritually mature. For me personally, I've experienced the greatest spiritual growth during the most difficult trials in my life.

So I encourage you to see challenges as opportunities for perseverance and spiritual growth. In these times, purposely pray more often, listen to the Lord, and read God's word daily so you can develop a closer relationship with God.

15. It's Never Too Late to Learn God's Way of Managing Money

For those who believe in God, he has promised to meet our needs as we put him first—no matter the difficulties we face. In Philippians 4:19, Paul said, "My God will meet all your needs according to the riches of his glory in Christ Jesus."

Note that Christ promised to meet our needs, but not necessarily our wants and desires.

Most people spend money on wants and desires as opposed to needs; this often leads to accumulating significant debt and having little or no savings. In order to get their finances in order, people in this situation will have to eliminate unnecessary spending.

God warned about the dangers of debt and admonished us to plan ahead and save for future needs (Proverbs 21:20). If you have not followed God's financial principles, then I want to encourage you that it's never too late to learn to manage money God's way. The solution is to study and implement God's financial principles, pray, and trust the Lord to direct you (Psalm 25:12).

16. God Promised to Protect Us

Throughout Psalm 91, God promised to protect us in many ways and instructed us not to fear a plague. Psalm 91:7–11 says:

> A thousand may fall at your side, ten thousand at your right hand, but it will not come near you. You will only observe with your eyes and see the punishment of the wicked. If you say, "The LORD is my refuge," and you make the Most High your dwelling, no harm will overtake you, no disaster will come near your tent. For he will command his angels concerning you to guard you in all your ways.

And two of my favourite verses in Psalm 91, verses 14–15, say, "'Because he loves me,' says the LORD, 'I will rescue him; I will protect him, for he acknowledges my name. He will call on me, and I will answer him; I will be with him in trouble, I will deliver him and honor him.'"

I encourage you to meditate upon God's promises in Psalm 91 and trust the God of the universe to protect you from whatever difficulties you face. Experience God's peace so you can make wise, biblically based financial decisions.

17. Fear Can Be Disabling: It's Better to Trust God

Any severe recession or financial crisis creates tremendous worldwide fear. Every day, there can be discouraging news in the media—lots of people are out of work with too much debt and are unable to pay their bills. Fear causes *many* to make hasty and unwise financial decisions. Others are so paralyzed with fear they are unable to make needed financial decisions.

In Matthew 6:25–27, Jesus said:

> "Therefore I tell you, do not worry about your life, what you will eat or drink; or about your body, what you will wear. Is not life more than food, and the body more than clothes? Look at the birds of the air; they do not sow or reap or store away in barns, and yet your heavenly Father feeds them. Are you not much more valuable than they? Can any one of you by worrying add a single hour to your life?"

Christ is telling us not to worry but to trust him, and God will provide for our needs.

18. Replace Your Fears With Trust in God

Remember God is always with you, regardless of what's happening in the world and regardless of what's happening with your personal finances—even if you just lost your job, or the mortgage company is threatening to take your home. In a crisis, David prayed to the Lord, "Even though I walk through the valley of the shadow of death, I will fear no evil, for you are with me; your rod and your staff, they comfort me" (Psalm 23:4, ESV).

When the Philistines had captured David, this was his prayer: "When I am afraid, I put my trust in you. In God, whose word I praise—in God I trust and am not afraid" (Psalm 56:3–4). If you are still worried about difficult circumstances, meditate upon

Psalm 55:22, which says: "Cast your cares on the LORD and he will sustain you; he will never let the righteous be shaken."

And here is one final Scripture to meditate upon in order to obtain God's peace. Proverbs 3:5–6 says, "Trust in the LORD with all your heart and lean not on your own understanding; in all your ways submit to him, and he will make your paths straight."

19. Be Strong and of Good Courage Regardless of the Difficulties

Are you afraid of downturns in the economy or hyperinflation where the cost of living becomes unbearable or a stock market crash that causes you to lose a significant portion of your retirement fund?

If you're worried about these things, I encourage you to consider God's instruction and promise to Joshua when he was about to become the leader of the Israelites. God said, "Be strong and courageous. Do not be afraid or terrified because of them, for the LORD your God goes with you; he will never leave you nor forsake you" (Deuteronomy 31:6).

As Christians, we need to demonstrate strength and courage as we face financial problems due to unexpected challenges. The opposite to fear is faith. We need to have faith in God that he will meet our needs (Philippians 4:19) and protect us (Psalm 91:5–11).

Many people are fearful, but as Christians, we need to replace fear with faith and trust in God, who created everything within six days and who is in total control. Psalm 103:19 states, "The LORD has established his throne in heaven, and his kingdom rules over all."

20. In Whom or in What Do You Trust?

The incredible uncertainty the world faced throughout the COVID-19 pandemic is one example that reveals to us what we really trust in. Do you trust in your steady job? Do you trust in your investments? Do you trust the government to provide for your needs? Or do you really trust in God?

Psalm 20:7 says, "Some trust in chariots and some in horses, but we trust in the name of the LORD our God." Financial crises or health crises, no matter how they arise, can really test the faith of Christians and reveal to us what we put our trust and hope in. For many, our trust is money and material things.

But of course, God has a different perspective. He wants us to trust solely in him at all times (Proverbs 3:5–6) because he is the King of kings the Lord of lords. Consider Romans 15:13, which states, "May the God of hope fill you with all joy and peace as you trust in him, so that you may overflow with hope by the power of the Holy Spirit."

21. Opportunity for Christians to Witness to Others

When a crisis strikes, most people are very worried about their health and their finances. Crises like market crashes, bad recessions, and pandemics prove that humans are not in control. We do not have all the answers; only God does. Isaiah 46:9–11 states:

> "Remember the former things, those of long ago; I am God, and there is no other; I am God, and there is none like me. I make known the end from the beginning, from ancient times, what is still to come. I say, 'My purpose will stand, and I will do all that I please.' From the east I summon a bird of prey; from a far-off land, a man to fulfill my

purpose. What I have said, that I will bring about; what I have planned, that I will do."

When crises arise, whether they're worldwide or centered on a particular country or a particular person, history has shown that during times of great trials, many people turn to God for answers and accept Jesus Christ as Saviour and Lord.

This means events like pandemics can be great opportunities for Christians to witness to non-Christians—telling them how Christ died on the cross and paid the penalty for their sins so that if they believe, they too can have eternal life. As 1 John 5:13 says, "I write these things to you who believe in the name of the Son of God so that you may know that you have eternal life."

Think about it: what could be more important than an individual's salvation, which lasts for eternity? The money and material things we have will be of no use to us a split second after we die (1 Timothy 6:7).

22. Psalm 23 Can Help Us Through Difficulties

The fear and anxiety arising from frightening situations can make you feel like you're going through a dark valley. I encourage you to pray as David did, "The LORD is my shepherd; I shall not want. He makes me to lie down in green pastures; He leads me beside the still waters. He restores my soul" (Psalm 23:1–3, NKJV).

In other words, God promised to shepherd us, provide for our needs, and restore us. David continues, "Though I walk through the valley of the shadow of death, I will fear no evil; for You are with me; Your rod and Your staff, they comfort me" (Psalm 23:4, NKJV).

David feared no evil, regardless of the valley, because God was with him and guiding him. Psalm 23 continues, "You anoint my head with oil; My cup runs over. Surely goodness and mercy shall follow me all the days of my life; And I will dwell in the house of the LORD forever" (Psalm 23:5–6, NKJV).

God will heal us, comfort us, and bless us in heaven with him forever. Praise the Lord!

23. Learn from Difficult Times

Most people are totally financially unprepared for a job loss arising from unexpected crises. They spend more than they earn and accumulate debt and have no savings. These things are contrary to Scripture (Proverbs 22:7; Proverbs 21:20).

If this is your situation, rather than getting down or angry about your financial problems, I encourage you to take this opportunity to learn God's way of managing money. This includes developing and implementing a budget to ensure you spend less than you earn and have a surplus to pay down debt and save for future needs.

As a minimum, I recommend that you save about six to nine months' worth of income, just in case you or your spouse are ever out of work. And learn the difference between a worldly perspective and a biblical perspective on money and material things. Most Christians unknowingly have a worldly perspective on money because they have never done an in-depth study of what the Bible says about finances. Benefit from trials by becoming better at managing money according to biblical principles.

24. Rejoice in the Lord Rather Than Worry About Difficulties

When COVID-19 spread in early 2020, there was negative news in the media every day. Increasing numbers of people were catching the virus, and many were dying. The government shut down many businesses; millions of people were out of work. Most people were discouraged, and some were depressed.

However, in Philippians 4:4–7, Paul provided this beneficial instruction.

Rejoice in the Lord always. I will say it again: Rejoice! Let your gentleness be evident to all. The Lord is near. Do not be anxious about anything, but in every situation, by prayer and petition, with thanksgiving, present your requests to God. And the peace of God, which transcends all understanding, will guard your hearts and your minds in Christ Jesus.

God promises his peace, regardless of the trials you're facing. Praise God!

Further on in this passage, Paul said, "Finally, brothers and sisters, whatever is true, whatever is noble, whatever is right, whatever is pure, whatever is lovely, whatever is admirable—if anything is excellent or praiseworthy—think about such things" (Philippians 4:8).

I recommend that you focus on prayer and God's blessings in your life, not on negative news in the media.

25. Allow Jesus to Carry the Heavy Part of the Load

Are you experiencing a difficult time and burdened and worried about your finances? In Matthew 11:28–29, Jesus said, "Come to me, all you who are weary and burdened, and I will give you rest. Take my yoke upon you and learn from me, for I am gentle and humble in heart, and you will find rest for your souls."

Jesus encourages us to come to him, asking for his help, and yoking ourselves with him—that is, depending on God to carry the heavy part of the load. When difficulties come, such as losing a job, we need to accept Christ's invitation and depend on him to carry the heavy part of our financial burden. Isaiah 46:4

says, "Even to your old age and gray hairs I am he, I am he who will sustain you. I have made you and I will carry you; I will sustain you and I will rescue you."

I encourage you—do not give up. Depend on God to carry you through any financial challenges you're facing.

26. Overwhelmed by Financial Problems

Do you feel overwhelmed by financial problems? Here are some practical steps to reduce your financial stress.

1. Review your bank and credit card statements to determine where you have been spending your money for the past six months.
2. Develop a budget to ensure you spend less than you earn so that you have a monthly surplus. Eliminate unnecessary expenses.
3. Use that surplus to pay down your most expensive debt first; this usually means your credit card debt. After that, pay down your other debts.
4. Save some money for emergencies. Proverbs 21:20 says, "The wise store up choice food and olive oil, but fools gulp theirs down."

And most importantly, spend quality time with the Lord daily, asking God for his wisdom and direction in managing money. In Isaiah 48:17, God promised, "I am the LORD your God, who teaches you what is best for you, who directs you in the way you should go."

27. God Will Bring Good Out of Financial Problems

Regardless of how difficult our financial problems are, God can solve them—either quickly or slowly. As indicated in Isaiah 46:9–

13 and many other Scriptures, God is in control. He is the King of kings and Lord of lords.

God has a purpose for every trial in the believer's life, including times of trial. He will bring some good out of every hardship. Romans 8:28 says, "We know that in all things God works for the good of those who love him, who have been called according to his purpose."

For example, we often grow more spiritually during trials, and God draws us closer to him. Because God is in control and he loves us, we know we can trust he will only allow those financial trials that are within his will.

God will provide the wisdom, direction, and strength we need to endure any trial. Psalm 46:1 says, "God is our refuge and strength, an ever-present help in trouble."

In summary, as you go through financial trials, ask God to reveal to you the purpose of those trials, and then respond accordingly.

28. So Stressed Out You Don't Want to Pray

Are you so stressed by financial problems that you don't know what to do, and you don't know what to pray to God?

First, remember you're not alone. Jesus said, "Never will I leave you; never will I forsake you" (Hebrews 13:5). Secondly, don't worry; rather, spend time with the Lord, and allow God, through his Holy Spirit, to pray on your behalf. Romans 8:26 says, "The Spirit helps us in our weakness. We do not know what we ought to pray for, but the Spirit himself intercedes for us through wordless groans."

Thirdly, ask God to comfort you. Paul said, "Praise be to the God and Father of our Lord Jesus Christ, the Father of compassion and the God of all comfort, who comforts us in all our troubles, so that we can comfort those in any trouble with the comfort we ourselves receive from God" (2 Corinthians 1:3–4).

In summary, spend time with the Lord, and allow God to comfort you and speak to you.

29. Are You Under Financial Stress and Don't Know What to Do?

If you are under financial stress because of a difficult situation and you don't know what to do, here's some biblically based advice.

Spend quality time with the Lord in prayer, reading his word on finances and asking him to speak to you through his word and Spirit. Hebrews 4:12 says, "The word of God is alive and active. Sharper than any double-edged sword, it penetrates even to dividing soul and spirit, joints and marrow; it judges the thoughts and attitudes of the heart."

Depend on God (John 15:5), and seek his wisdom (James 1:5) and specific direction (Psalm 32:8) in making any future financial decisions. And be sure to have Jesus's mindset, saying, "Father, if you are willing, take this cup from me; yet not my will, but yours be done" (Luke 22:42).

If you do these things, then God will direct you in making the wisest financial decision. Psalm 25:12 says, "Who, then, are those who fear the LORD? He will instruct them in the ways they should choose."

30. Lord, Why All of These Financial Problems?

Are you experiencing severe financial problems due to unforeseen difficulties? If yes, consider 1 Peter 1:6–7:

> Though now for a little while you may have had to suffer grief in all kinds of trials. These have come so that the

proven genuineness of your faith—of greater worth than gold, which perishes even though refined by fire—may result in praise, glory and honor when Jesus Christ is revealed.

Financial and other problems may be extremely difficult. But when you continue to trust the Lord, your faith is proven genuine and is of greater worth than gold (this includes money and material things).

Paul assured us, "Our light and momentary troubles are achieving for us an eternal glory that far outweighs them all. So we fix our eyes not on what is seen, but on what is unseen, since what is seen is temporary, but what is unseen is eternal" (2 Corinthians 4:17–18).

In other words, do not focus on money and material things, which are temporary. Rather, focus on the rewards that God will bestow upon Christians for eternity when they continue to put their faith and trust in God, notwithstanding their severe financial difficulties.

31. Are You Hurting Emotionally Because of Difficulties?

Are you hurting emotionally because of financial problems caused by hard times? Do you feel broken-hearted or oppressed? If yes, then don't worry. Jesus has this wonderful promise for you!

"The Spirit of the LORD is upon Me, because He has anointed Me to preach the gospel to the poor; He has sent Me to heal the brokenhearted, to proclaim liberty to the captives and recovery of sight to the blind, to set at liberty those who are oppressed." (Luke 4:18, NKJV)

Remember, God is with you and has promised to help you. Psalm 34:18 says, "The LORD is close to the brokenhearted and saves those who are crushed in spirit." And in Isaiah 40:31, God said, "Those who hope in the LORD will renew their strength. They will soar on wings like eagles; they will run and not grow weary, they will walk and not be faint."

The most practical way to experience God's hope and comfort during times of financial difficulty is to meditate on key Scriptures, such as those above. "This is my comfort in my misery, that Your word has revived me" (Psalm 119:50, NASB).

32. Are You Experiencing Financial Problems Due to Difficult Times?

Have you accumulated significant debt? If yes, I encourage you to draw close to the Lord in prayer. Meditate on key Scriptures that apply to finances, and allow God to direct you through his word. Psalm 119:105 says: "your word is a lamp for my feet, a light on my path."

Since 1982, I've counselled thousands of people who were in so much debt their situations looked impossible. However, once they learned to manage money according to biblical financial principles, God provided little miracles. For example, some received unexpected income or found great deals on purchases; others learned to be content with less, and the Lord provided for their financial needs, enabling them to pay down their debts.

Here are two references to God's provision in Scripture. In 2 Kings 4:1–7, God miraculously provided oil to a widow and her son so she could pay all their debts. And in Matthew 6, Christ promised if we put him first, he will meet our needs!

In summary, if you are experiencing financial problems, draw close to the Lord in prayer, meditate upon key Scriptures, and allow God to direct you through his word and his spirit. God will provide what you need (Philippians 4:19)!

To learn more about managing money during difficult times, go to www.coplandfinancialministries.org and watch the numerous videos on that topic. In addition, if you would like to do develop and implement a budget to ensure that you have a positive cash flow each month to pay down debt and save for future needs, then be sure to download a free copy of the Copland budgeting system and watch the videos explaining how to use the budgeting system.

XIII.
GOD PROVIDES MIRACULOUSLY

1. God Provides Through Elijah

In this section, I'm going to provide examples of where God has met needs miraculously. In 1 Kings 17, there is a story of how God met the needs of a widow and her son during a severe drought. The drought had lasted for years, and the widow's food was almost gone.

Her situation was so desperate that she believed that she and her son would die. However, Elijah encouraged her not to be afraid but to trust God to meet her needs. This widow had enough faith to give the man of God, Elijah, some bread even when she had so little. God honoured her faith by meeting her needs.

1 Kings 17:15–16 says, "There was food every day for Elijah and for the woman and her family. For the jar of flour was not used up and the jug of oil did not run dry, in keeping with the word of the LORD spoken by Elijah."

In conclusion, manage money and material possessions according to God's will, and he will meet your needs.

2. Jesus Feeds the Five Thousand

In the story in Luke 9:12–17, thousands of people had come to hear Jesus speak. Jesus taught them about the kingdom of God and healed many.

Late in the afternoon the Twelve came to him and said, "Send the crowd away so they can go to the surrounding villages and countryside and find food and lodging, because we are in a remote place here."

He replied, "You give them something to eat."

They answered, "We have only five loaves of bread and two fish—unless we go and buy food for all this crowd."

About five thousand men were there. Clearly, the disciples did not have the resources to feed the people. Jesus miraculously multiplied the food and fed about five thousand men and there were twelve basketfuls of broken pieces left over (Luke 9:17).

Clearly, Jesus has the power to meet your financial needs, either miraculously or in a normal way. So be sure to manage money God's way, and pray, trusting him to meet your needs. In Philippians 4:19, Paul said, "My God will meet all your needs according to the riches of his glory in Christ Jesus."

3. Elisha and the Widow's Oil

In 2 Kings 4, we have the story of a widow who is about to lose her two boys as slaves because of debts owed by her and her late husband. She appealed for help to the prophet Elisha, who gave her instructions to obtain many jars from her neighbours, then go inside, shut the door, and pour the oil into jars.

God did a miracle as he took the little bit of oil that she had and multiplied it tremendously so that she had many jars of oil. At that time, oil was very valuable. Elisha instructed her, "Go, sell the oil and pay your debts. You and your sons can live on what is left" (2 Kings 4:7).

I encourage you, if you are in a lot of debt, God is able to help you get out of debt. Sometimes he will do it quickly, but generally, he does it slowly so we can learn whatever lessons he may have for us, including learning to trust him even more.

4. God Provides for the Temple

In 1 Chronicles 29, God performed a miracle as he moved in the heart of King David and the people to give extremely generously and willingly to the building of God's spectacular temple. Of interest, there is no indication that they borrowed money in order to build the temple. Rather, everyone gave generously, and no debt was used. After the temple was constructed, David did not get puffed up with pride. In 1 Chronicles 29:10–14, it says:

> David praised the LORD in the presence of the whole assembly, saying, "Praise be to you, LORD, the God of our father Israel, from everlasting to everlasting. Yours, LORD, is the greatness and the power and the glory and the majesty and the splendor, for everything in heaven and earth is yours ... Wealth and honor come from you; you are the ruler of all things ... Now, our God, we give you thanks, and praise your glorious name. But who am I, and who are my people, that we should be able to give as generously as this? Everything comes from you, and we have given you only what comes from your hand."

In light of the above and many other examples in the Bible, Christians should trust God to meet their needs.

5. God Provides a Church Building for New Congregation

Since 1982, I've seen many churches take on significant amounts of debt for building expansions. Of interest, regarding all the temples and tabernacles that were built in Scripture, there is no indication anywhere that debt was taken on.

In Deuteronomy 28, God promised his people that if they fully obeyed him, they would not have to borrow. In other words, God would meet their needs without incurring debt (Philippians 4:19).

Impossible, you say? Several years ago, there was a new and fast-growing congregation in my area that had been renting different facilities. The leaders and members prayed fervently and waited upon the Lord, and God miraculously provided them with a church building and property at no cost. It was given to them by another congregation whose membership had shrunk very significantly and whose leaders wanted the building to be better utilized for God's work.

Ephesians 3:20–21 states, "Now to him who is able to do immeasurably more than all we ask or imagine, according to his power that is at work within us, to him be glory in the church and in Christ Jesus throughout all generations."

6. Elisha Raises the Shunammite's Son

In the Old Testament, most women depended on men to provide money for food and other necessities. So it was important that a woman have a son who could provide for her in her old age.

In 2 Kings 4, the Shunammite woman was worried because she had no son and her husband was old. She was a godly woman who had provided a place for Elisha to stay. Elisha asked what he could do for her, and she said she wanted a son. Elisha prophesied she would have a son within one year. Even though she had her doubts, God answered that prayer and she gave birth to a son.

Several years later, the son died. The Shunammite woman believed God could heal her son, so she travelled some distance and found Elisha. He prayed over the boy, and God miraculously brought the son back to life. In this way, her future financial needs were met.

In summary, if you put God first, he will meet your needs—sometimes through normal ways and sometimes miraculously.

7. God Provides a Car Miraculously

I've seen many cases where a Christian needed a car and God provided it in a miraculous way. Here are two examples.

Several years ago, I reviewed the finances of a single mom and helped her develop a budget. Her car was worn out, and she needed to replace it, but she could not afford a car loan. I encouraged her to prayerfully claim Christ's promise in Matthew 6 that God will meet our needs if we put him first. Within two months, someone from her church gave her a car that was in really good shape.

I think of a similar situation with a couple involved in full-time ministry. They could not afford to purchase a car, so they prayed, and God directed a fellow Christian to give them a car.

In both of these cases, if the individuals had not prayed and waited upon the Lord for his provision, they could have missed out on God's blessings. Isaiah 64:4 states, "Since ancient times no one has heard, no ear has perceived, no eye has seen any God besides you, *who acts on behalf of those who wait for him*" (emphasis added).

In summary, if you have a need, take it before the Lord in prayer, wait upon him for his timing (Psalm 37:7), and then trust God to act on your behalf in meeting your needs.

8. God Enables People to Pay Off Debt

Here is a common example of God enabling his people to pay off debt. When one couple attended my in-depth series called "Financial Management God's Way," they had a big mortgage, two car loans, a personal line of credit, and significant credit card debt. Like many people, they had been unknowingly violating many biblical financial principles.

After they learned and applied God's word on finances, God provided several small miracles, including some unexpected income and wisdom in reducing expenses. They also learned to be content with less (Philippians 4:11–13).

The couple downsized their lifestyle and implemented a budget to ensure they had a surplus each month. Within three years they had paid off their credit cards, the personal line of credit, and the two car loans.

They continued to manage money God's way, and seven years later, they paid off their mortgage and were totally debt-free. When God called the husband into full-time ministry, they were able to accept the ministry job with a lesser salary because they had followed God's financial principles.

On the other hand, if they had managed money the way most people do, they would have been "a servant to the lender" (Proverbs 22:7). In that case, the husband would have had to continue in his better-paying job in order to service their debts. He would not have had the option to go into full-time ministry. Debt often limits an individual's or a couple's future options.

9. God Provides for the Tabernacle

Exodus 35 to 36 provides the story of Moses leading the people to build a tabernacle for the Lord. What's interesting is that Moses did not put people under pressure. Rather, he just encouraged those who were willing to give to the Lord's tabernacle (Exodus 35:5).

Some people brought various types of materials, and some used their skills to help with the construction of the tabernacle. Exodus 35:21 states, "Everyone who was willing and whose heart moved them came and brought an offering to the LORD."

What's amazing is this: God did a miracle as he moved in the people's hearts so strongly that they gave so generously. No debt was used.

> Then Moses gave an order and they sent this word throughout the camp: "No man or woman is to make anything else as an offering for the sanctuary." And so the people were restrained from bringing more, because what they already had was more than enough to do all the work. (Exodus 36:6–7)

In summary, God can move in people's hearts to give generously if they are willing, and the work can be done without debt.

10. God Provides Fish for Peter

In Luke 5:4–9, Jesus said:

> "Put out into deep water, and let down the nets for a catch."
> Simon answered, "Master, we've worked hard all night and haven't caught anything. But because you say so, I will let down the nets."
> When they had done so, they caught such a large number of fish that their nets began to break. So they signaled their partners in the other boat to come and help them, and they came and filled both boats so full that they began to sink.
> When Simon Peter saw this, he fell at Jesus's knees and said, "Go away from me, Lord; I am a sinful man!" For he and all his companions were astonished at the catch of fish they had taken.

Simon Peter was an experienced fisherman. Fishing was his expertise, while Jesus was a carpenter before he began his ministry. Simon Peter could have easily refused to follow Jesus's instructions. He could have said something like "No, Jesus, it doesn't make sense to fish in the daytime. Remember, fishing is my expertise; your expertise is carpentry." However, Peter did not respond that way. Instead, he did what Jesus said.

In order to be blessed by the Lord, Peter had to obey God's instructions (Acts 5:29), trust God's wisdom rather than his own understanding (Proverbs 3:5–6), and take specific action as God directed him (James 1:22).

I encourage you to trust and obey God's instructions and take specific action as he directs you so that you can also be blessed by the Lord.

11. God Provides Bread and Water to the Israelites

In Exodus 16, God demonstrated his incredible power by providing miracles on a daily basis. The Israelites were in the desert and had no food, but God intervened and provided them with quail in the evenings and manna in the mornings (Exodus 16:8). God demonstrated his power by performing these miracles regularly for forty years while the Israelites were in the desert.

We know that Christ promised to meet our needs as we put him first (Matthew 6:31–33). Over the years, I've seen numerous cases where God has continuously provided for his people. Yes, sometimes there are miracles, but most of the time God provides opportunities for us to work to earn a living or meets our needs with the help of a fellow believer.

In summary, pray regularly, do as the Lord directs you, and trust God to meet your needs. In Philippians 4:19, Paul said, "My God will meet all your needs according to the riches of his glory in Christ Jesus."

12. God Provides Little Miracles

As well as providing incredible miracles, sometimes God provides little miracles or teaches us to manage money better. Many Christians unknowingly manage money the world's way. They spend more than they earn and accumulate debt because they have limited knowledge of God's word on finances.

However, once they learn and start to apply biblical financial principles, often God's hand will start to move and provide little miracles. It could be unexpected income or wisdom in reducing expenses; it might be a new job, or God could teach them to be content with less (Philippians 4:11–13).

One thing is clear, that as we put God first, he will meet our needs. Jesus said:

> "Do not worry, saying, 'What shall we eat? or 'What shall we drink?' or 'What shall we wear?' For the pagans run after all these things, and your heavenly Father knows that you need them. But seek first his kingdom and his righteousness, and all these things will be given to you as well." (Matthew 6:31–33)

In summary, study and apply God's financial principles in managing the money he has entrusted to you, and the Lord will meet your needs!

Go to www.coplandfinancialministries.org to learn more about God's word on finances. We have numerous resources there, most of which are free. You can also follow @biblefinance on Facebook, Instagram, and Twitter.

XIV.
DISCERNING GOD'S WILL

1. God Wants Us to Understand His Will

In Ephesians 5:15–17, Paul said, "Be very careful, then, how you live—not as unwise but as wise, making the most of every opportunity, because the days are evil. Therefore do not be foolish, but understand what the Lord's will is."

Does God have a specific will for his children? Yes! The Bible is clear that God wants to direct us according to his will. For example, in Psalm 32:8, God said, "I will instruct you and teach you in the way you should go; I will counsel you with my loving eye on you."

In Psalm 25:12, God promised, "Who, then, are those who fear the LORD? He will instruct them in the ways they should choose."

And in Jeremiah 29:11, God provided this wonderful promise. "'For I know the plans I have for you,' declares the LORD, 'plans to prosper you and not to harm you, plans to give you hope and a future.'"

Scripture is clear that God wants us to discern his specific will before we make any important decision including financial decisions.

2. Don't Miss God's Blessings!

Bill and Sue needed to replace their car. Unfortunately, like most people, Bill and Sue did not pray and ask God to provide. Rather, they borrowed the money and bought a new car because the loan was so readily available, and they figured that, at zero per cent financing, it was a good deal.

Unknown to Bill and Sue, someone at their church—who was aware of their tight financial situation—had planned to give them his good used car. However, because they acted without consulting the Lord, Bill and Sue missed God's blessing.

Everyone should follow Jehoshaphat's instructions: "First seek the counsel of the LORD" (1 Kings 22:5). We should pray and give God a chance to provide before moving ahead depending upon our own limited knowledge. In Philippians 4:19, Paul said, "My God will meet all your needs according to the riches of his glory in Christ Jesus."

Before making any important financial decision, the wise Christian prayerfully seeks God's direction (Psalm 25:12) and waits for God's timing. "Rest in the LORD, and wait patiently for him" (Psalm 37:7, KJV).

3. Review God's Word

God's word often provides clear direction for making financial decisions. Here are some examples:

1. Save for future needs. Proverbs 21:20 says, "The wise store up choice food and olive oil, but fools gulp theirs down."
2. Use minimal debt because Proverbs 22:7 warns of the dangers of debt.
3. Put God first in managing money, and he will meet your needs. In Philippians 4:19, Paul said, "My God will meet all your needs according to the riches of his glory in Christ Jesus."
4. Do not covet what others have. Exodus 20:17 states, "You shall not covet your neighbor's house. You shall not covet your neighbor's wife, or his male or female

servant, his ox or donkey, or anything that belongs to your neighbor."

5. And learn to be content with God's provision. Paul said:

I have learned to be content whatever the circumstances. I know what it is to be in need, and I know what it is to have plenty. I have learned the secret of being content in any and every situation, whether well fed or hungry, whether living in plenty or in want. I can do all this through him who gives me strength. (Philippians 4:11–13)

In summary, in order to discern God's will in managing money, you should review and follow God's financial principles as provided in his word.

4. Take an Eternal Perspective, Not a Temporal One

In order to discern God's specific will, it's important to take an eternal perspective, not a temporal one. In Colossians 3:1–2, Paul said, "Since, then, you have been raised with Christ, set your hearts on things above, where Christ is, seated at the right hand of God. Set your minds on things above, not on earthly things."

In other words, make the paradigm shift from focusing on the temporal (such as money and material things) to focusing on things of eternal value, such as your relationship with Christ, quality time with your spouse and children, involvement in ministry, and investing money in God's kingdom.

Remember, Jesus said, "It is more blessed to give than to receive" (Acts 20:35). When your heart and mind are focused on things of eternal value, it's much more likely you will be able to discern God's specific will in any financial decision.

5. The Bible Provides Financial Guidelines

The Bible provides incredible wisdom on how to manage money. However, sometimes there are several options within God's financial principles. In these circumstances, a Christian needs to discern God's specific will as to which option they should choose.

In order to discern God's specific will, there is no substitute for having a close personal relationship with the Lord Jesus Christ. This is because, as you prayerfully seek God's wisdom and direction, he will speak to you through his word (Psalm 119:105) and Spirit (John 10:27).

In conclusion, when you're facing an important financial decision, review God's financial principles as provided in his word, determine the various options within those guidelines, and then take the time to specifically discern exactly what God wants you to do. And be sure to adopt Jesus's mindset when he said to the Father, "Yet not my will, but yours be done" (Luke 22:42).

6. Real-Life Example: Rob and Pam Discern God's Will

Rob and Pam are a young couple who have been managing money God's way. During their prayer times, they sense God's leading to purchase a house. Many questions arise. Should they buy a four-bedroom or three-bedroom house? How much should they spend? What is the maximum they should borrow?

There are several options within God's financial principles. To discern God's specific will, they should start with the following actions. In prayer, ask God for his wisdom (James 1:5) and specific direction (Psalm 32:8), which God has promised to provide (Isaiah 48:17).

Next, review God's word on finances and allow the Lord, through his Holy Spirit, to highlight Scriptures to specifically direct them. Psalm 119:105 says, "Your word is a lamp for my feet and a light for my path."

Be patient and wait for God's timing and peace (John 14:27) with respect to a particular house purchase. Lamentations 3:24 says, "The LORD is my portion; therefore I will wait for him."

7. Acknowledge You Are a Steward of God's Resources

To determine God's specific will for any major financial decision, you need to acknowledge in your heart and mind that you are a steward of God's resources. God is the owner!

Psalm 24:1–2 says: "The earth is the LORD's and everything in it, the world, and all who live in it." And Haggai 2:8 says, "'The silver is mine and the gold is mine,' declares the LORD Almighty."

If you believe you are an owner, consider what Ecclesiastes 5:15 says: "Everyone comes naked from their mother's womb, and as everyone comes, so they depart. They take nothing from their toil that they can carry in their hands." In other words, a split second after you die, you will realize you were just a steward or manager of God's resources for the relatively short time (compared to eternity) that you are here on earth.

So, as stewards of God's money and material things, we need to look to the owner (God) for how we should use his resources.

8. Remember, God Gave You the Ability to Earn Income

In order to discern God's will in any major financial decision, we need to understand that we are stewards, not owners of money and material things. Many of us have worked hard exercising our skills and abilities to earn our incomes, and therefore, we may believe that we can spend "our money" as we please. After all, we earned it.

However, I encourage you to consider who gave you your skills and abilities. Deuteronomy 8:17–18 is clear, "You may say to yourself, 'My power and the strength of my hands have produced this wealth for me.' But remember the LORD your God, for it is he who gives you the ability to produce wealth."

Since it is God who gave all of your natural abilities, including the ability to earn a good income, you should look to the Lord for how you should spend the money he has entrusted to you.

9. Understand That You Are Accountable to God

In the parable of the talents (Matthew 25:14–30), the master, who represents God, entrusted different amounts of money to three different servants. To one servant, he entrusted five talents; to a second servant, two talents; to a third servant, one talent.

Scripture says that "after a long time" (perhaps a lifetime?) God returned and made the servants accountable to him. Similarly, God has entrusted different levels of income to his children. So regardless of your income, you are accountable to God for how you use his money. Romans 14:12 says, "Each of us will give an account of ourselves to God."

And 1 Corinthians 4:2 says, "It is required that those who have been given a trust must prove faithful." Faithfulness to God is the key, so we need to manage money according to his principles and discern his specific will before we make any major financial decision.

10. Pray and Ask God for His Wisdom and Specific Direction

Since only God knows the future (Isaiah 46:10) and only God is in control (Psalm 103:19), everyone needs God's wisdom in managing money. James 1:5–6 instructs us, "If any of you lacks wisdom, you should ask God, who gives generously to all without finding fault, and it will be given to you. But when you ask, you must believe and not doubt."

Note that you need to have enough faith to believe God will provide his wisdom. Hebrews 11:6 confirms this. "And without faith it is impossible to please God, because anyone who comes to him must believe that he exists and that he rewards those who earnestly seek him." Jesus said, "Blessed rather are those who hear the word of God and obey it" (Luke 11:28).

In summary, pray and trust God to give you his wisdom and specific direction before making any major financial decision.

11. Sometimes, God's Answer Is "No" or "Wait"

Over the years, I've met many Christians who will pray and ask God for something. But they do not invest the time in communication with the Lord in order to discern his specific will, which is God's best for them in that situation.

Sometimes, God's best is a "no" because we have asked for something that is not good for us long-term. At other times, God's answer is "wait"; our request may be appropriate, but the timing isn't right.

Isaiah 64:4 says, "No eye has seen any God besides you, who acts on behalf of those who wait for him." In other words, at the appropriate time, God will act on your behalf in accordance with his specific will, which is always in your best interest. God loves us unconditionally, and he always has his best in mind for us. Jeremiah 31:3 says that the Lord loves us with an everlasting love.

So when you pray, be sure to ask God for his wisdom and specific direction so that you can discern his will and not your own will. As Jesus said to the Father, "Yet not my will, but yours be done" (Luke 22:42).

12. God Is Interested in Your Financial Decisions!

So often, Christians believe God is not interested in their financial decisions, and therefore, they need to make decisions based upon their own judgment and experience, without consulting the Lord. But this is not true! God is very interested in all of our decisions including financial decisions.

In Isaiah 48:17, God gives us this awesome promise of His guidance. "I am the LORD your God, who teaches you what is best for you, who directs you in the way you should go." And Proverbs 3:5–6 says, "Trust in the LORD with all your heart and lean not on your own understanding; in all your ways submit to him, and he will make your paths straight." In other words, God has promised to direct us in our decisions.

In summary, discerning and implementing God's will is by far the best option with respect to any major financial decision.

13. Obtain Biblical Counsel from a Godly Financial Adviser

As 1 Corinthians 2:14–15 says, "The person without the Spirit does not accept the things that come from the Spirit of God but considers them foolishness, and cannot understand them because they are discerned only through the Spirit. The person with the Spirit makes judgments about all things."

In my view, a godly financial adviser would be a spiritually mature Christian who understands and applies God's financial principles (Psalm 111:10), who has a close personal relationship with the Lord (John 15), who has the necessary practical financial knowledge (Proverbs 24:3–4), and who habitually puts the interests of clients first (Philippians 2:3–4).

With respect to finding a godly financial adviser, be careful. Unfortunately, most Christians have limited knowledge of what the Bible says about finances. As a result, they often give worldly financial advice and cannot teach you how to discern God's specific will.

In summary, find a godly financial adviser to help you discern God's specific will before you make any major financial decision.

14. Spiritual Discernment

As 1 Corinthians 2:14–15 says:

> The person without the Spirit does not accept the things that come from the Spirit of God but considers them foolishness, and cannot understand them because they are discerned only through the Spirit. The person with the Spirit makes judgments about all things.

In other words, if you want to discern God's will (that is, God's best) with respect to any important financial decision, such discernment can only come from the Spirit of God. You cannot figure it out on your own.

Spiritual discernment is available to all Christians who regularly invest the time to develop their relationship with the Lord. This generally requires habitually spending quality time with the Lord in prayer, meditating on God's word (Joshua 1:9), "sitting still before the Lord" (Psalm 46:10), and listening carefully for God's instructions (Psalm 25:12).

Jesus said, "My sheep listen to my voice; I know them, and they follow me" (John 10:27). God has never spoken to me audibly, although I believe he could, since he spoke to Moses audibly. However, God has certainly spoken to me through his word (Psalm 119:105) and his Holy Spirit, who lives within every Christian who has accepted Christ as Saviour and Lord. Psalm 25:12 says, "Who, then, are those who fear the LORD? He will instruct them in the ways they should choose."

In summary, purposely develop your relationship with the Lord so you can exercise spiritual discernment with respect to God's specific will for any important decision.

15. Top Priority: Develop Your Relationship With Christ

If you want to discern God's will (God's best) with respect to any important decision, it's critical that you develop a close relationship with the Lord. Jesus said, "Very truly I tell you, the Son can do nothing by himself; he can do only what he sees his Father doing, because whatever the Father does the Son also does" (John 5:19).

Because of Jesus's close relationship with God the Father, Jesus could sense where the Father was working and would follow the Father's lead. Similarly, God wants us to have such a close personal relationship with him so we can discern his directives rather than making important decisions based on our own judgments. Jesus's words "I know my sheep and my sheep know me" (John 10:14) refer to the intimate and personal relationship every Christian can have with God.

In summary, a close personal relationship with the Lord will enable you to hear God's voice (John 10:27) and guide you regarding any major financial decision.

16. Learn to Recognize God's Voice

Some Christians believe that as long as they are within God's financial guidelines, they can make the final decision without discerning the Lord's specific will. They only need to ask God to stop them if their decision is not God's will. This mindset of making financial decisions (and asking God to stop you if it's not his will) removes the necessity of developing a close relationship with the Lord, which is essential in making every important decision.

Here's a good analogy. If a close relative calls you on the phone and starts speaking, you would immediately recognize their voice. Why? Because you have a close and consistent relationship with them. Similarly, in order for us to recognize God's voice and discern God's will, we must develop and maintain a close personal relationship with the Lord.

Jesus said, "The gatekeeper opens the gate for him, and the sheep listen to his voice. He calls his own sheep by name and leads them out. When he has brought out all his own, he goes on ahead of them, and his sheep follow him because they know his voice" (John 10:3–4).

In summary, regularly take the time to develop your relationship with Christ so you can recognize God's voice when he is trying to direct you. God's voice can come in many forms. The Holy Spirit could highlight Scriptures as you read the Bible, God could give you his peace or lack of peace about a proposed financial decision, and he could speak to you through a godly financial adviser (Psalm 1:1–3).

17. Suggestions to Develop Your Relationship With God
Here are some suggestions to enable you to develop a close personal relationship with the Lord Jesus Christ.

1. First and foremost, you need to have accepted Jesus Christ as your Saviour and Lord.
2. Habitually spend quality time with the Lord in prayer, reading his word (2 Timothy 3:16–17) and allowing God, through his Spirit, to speak to your heart and mind. God can communicate to you by highlighting certain verses.
3. Be still before the Lord (Psalm 46:10), and listen to what he has to say to you through his Holy Spirit. Psalm 85:8 says, "I will listen to what God the LORD says."

4. Regularly attend a Bible-believing church where you can learn more about God's word, enjoy Christian fellowship, and seek biblical counsel (Hebrews 10:24).

5. Consistently work to develop your relationship with the Lord. In Jeremiah 29:12–13, God said, "Then you will call on me and come and pray to me, and I will listen to you. You will seek me and find me when you seek me with all your heart."

I encourage you to follow up on the above suggestions for developing a close relationship with the Lord. Some excellent resources that can help you in this regard are available at www.coplandfinancialministries.org. Also, be sure to watch the three half-hour videos titled "Discerning God's Will in Managing Money."

18. Ask God to Provide His Direction in Your Circumstances

During the workshops I do, this question often comes up: Can God direct me through my circumstances? The answer is yes, but there are some cautions.

God can open and close the appropriate doors, similar to what the Lord did for Gideon when he set out a fleece to seek God's direction (Judges 6:37–40).

However, in regard to assuming debt, be very careful. The availability of debt may be not an open door from God but rather a deception from Satan to tempt you to take on debt that is outside of God's will. This causes you to become "a slave to the lender" (Proverbs 22:7), leading to all kinds of financial stress.

In 1 Kings 3, Solomon asked for wisdom, and God said he would give him a "wise and discerning heart." That's what we all want because, as Ephesians 5:15–17 says, "Be very careful, then, how you live—not as unwise but as wise, making the most of every opportunity, because the days are evil. Therefore do not be foolish, but understand what the Lord's will is."

In summary, God can direct you by opening and closing doors. However, if you encounter an open door, before you proceed, determine if your proposed financial decision is consistent with God's word, and obtain some biblical financial counsel.

19. Be Careful of External Pressure

Sometimes, when you face a major financial decision, other people may pressure you to make the decision they believe is best for you. Or sometimes they may pressure you to make a decision that is best for them!

When either of these situations occurs, it is critical to make a decision that's in accordance with God's will, not someone else's desire. In Deuteronomy 28:2, God promised, "All these blessings will come on you and accompany you if you obey the LORD your God."

As Peter says, your highest priority is this. "We must obey God rather than human beings!" (Act 5:29). We are individually accountable to God, not to someone else. In Romans 14:12, Paul said, "Each of us will give an account of ourselves to God."

If in the process of making a major financial decision you feel external pressure from other people, be sure to ignore this "people pressure" and focus on your relationship with God. Read God's word, and seek biblical counsel, and God will direct you to make the best decision (Isaiah 48:17).

Go to www.coplandfinancialministries.org to learn more about God's word on finances. We have numerous resources there, most of which are free. You can also follow @biblefinance on Facebook, Instagram, and Twitter.

XV.
INVESTING GOD'S WAY

1. Pray and Depend on God for His Wisdom and Direction
The best investments today depend on future events, and because no human can consistently predict the direction of any market, it's critical to acknowledge our dependence upon God. James 4:13–15 says:

> Now listen, you who say, "Today or tomorrow we will go to this or that city, spend a year there, carry on business and make money." Why, you do not even know what will happen tomorrow. What is your life? You are a mist that appears for a little while and then vanishes. Instead, you ought to say, "If it is the Lord's will, we will live and do this or that."

The good news is that our all-knowing God *does* know the future (2 Kings 7:1), and he is willing to provide us with his wisdom (James 1:5) and direction in all aspects of life, including investing. "In all your ways acknowledge Him, and He shall direct your paths" (Proverbs 3:6, NKJV).

Therefore, if you want to invest money God's way, you must pray and depend on the Lord for his wisdom and direction.

2. Invest According to God's Specific Will
Our stewardship responsibility is to invest the money God has entrusted to us in accordance with his will. Here are some ways God can guide us.

1. God can speak to our hearts and minds through the Holy Spirit. Jesus said, "My sheep listen to My voice,

and I know them, and they follow Me" (John 10:27, NASB).

2. God will often direct us through his word. Psalm 119:105 says, "Your word is a lamp for my feet, a light on my path."

3. And God can provide his peace or lack of peace. Jesus said, "Peace I leave with you; my peace I give you" (John 14:27).

When you invest money according to God's will, you may not necessarily make the highest returns, but God will provide his peace and meet your future needs (Matthew 6:31–33).

In summary, prayerfully allow God through his Spirit and word to determine where you invest God's money.

3. Determine God's Will Before You Act

Often, we make investment decisions based on our own understanding or advice from others. Afterward, we pray and ask God to bless our decisions. This is contrary to God's word. Even Jesus said to the Father, "Yet not my will, but yours be done" (Luke 22:42).

God wants us to prayerfully determine his will in the planning stages before we make any important financial decisions. Indeed, God does have a plan! Jeremiah 29:11 says, "'For I know the plans I have for you,' declares the LORD, 'plans to prosper you and not to harm you, plans to give you hope and a future.'"

The key to knowing God's financial plan is to develop a close personal relationship with Jesus Christ. As you prayerfully listen for God's gentle whisper (1 Kings 19), you should be able to sense the promptings of the Holy Spirit and determine God's investment strategy.

In summary, before making any major financial decision, through prayer and the study of God's word, determine God's financial plan for you and your family.

4. God's Wisdom Avoids Bad Investments

God wants us to invest his money according to his investment principles, but unfortunately, most Christians have little or no knowledge of what the Bible says about investing. The majority of bad investments can be avoided if you understand and apply God's investment principles. Here are four examples:

1. Proverbs 19:2 recommends that you do not invest in something you don't understand.
2. In Proverbs 22:7, God discouraged debt because the use of debt increases the risk and volatility of your portfolio.
3. Proverbs 21:5 warns not to make hasty decisions because they are often the wrong decisions.
4. In Ecclesiastes 11:1–2, God recommended diversification in order to minimize risk and volatility.

Since God's word has so much wisdom on investing, the wise Christian learns and implements God's investment principles.

5. Follow a Biblically Based Investment Strategy

A biblically based investment strategy is one that is consistent with God's word and reflects his specific will. I suggest that you review your investment portfolio three to four times per year and spend quality time with the Lord in prayer and reading his word to sense his specific direction.

God promised, "I will instruct you and teach you in the way you should go; I will counsel you with my loving eye on you"

(Psalm 32:8). When you sense God's leading through his Spirit and word, be sure to write it down (Habakkuk 2:2).

Why? Because most people tend to respond to sales calls, hot tips, good ideas, etc. As a result, they make investment decisions on a case-by-case basis rather than developing a biblically based investment strategy that God has revealed to them.

In summary, develop and implement a biblically based investment strategy that reflects God's will regarding the investments that God has entrusted to you.

6. Invest in Several Categories

Because no human can consistently predict the direction of any market (James 4:11–13), it is important to diversify your assets into different categories of investments that will likely react differently to any given market condition.

Ecclesiastes 11:1–2 says, "Ship your grain across the sea; after many days you may receive a return. Invest in seven ventures, yes, in eight; you do not know what disaster may come upon the land."

"Ship your grain across the sea" was a metaphorical expression used in the grain trade to illustrate the potential successful prospects of a business investment. In other words, it is biblical to take some risk. However, God recommends diversifying your investments into seven or eight different categories because you do not know what the future holds. As a practical matter, diversification will reduce the risk and volatility of your portfolio.

In summary, God recommends diversification of the investments he has entrusted to you.

7. Diversify Your Investments

Over the past 44 years, I've seen too many cases where an individual has the majority of their investments in one company or in one sector. For a season, these investments may do well, but inevitably every company and sector falls on bad times. This results in significant losses because the portfolio was not biblically diversified.

Generally, these large losses can be avoided if the investments are diversified in accordance with Ecclesiastes 11:1–2. That way, if one category decreases in value, generally another category should be increasing, thus reducing the volatility and risk of your portfolio.

Many investors try "time-to-market." That is, they buy when they believe that the market is headed higher and sell when they believe the market is going lower. However, God says (and history shows) that we cannot consistently predict the future.

Proverbs 27:1 says, "Do not boast about tomorrow, for you do not know what a day may bring." The biblical truth is that whether you're a layperson or a professional money manager, absolutely no one can consistently predict the direction of the markets, so diversification is most important.

In summary, unless God specifically directs you otherwise (John 10:3–4), diversify your investments as Ecclesiastes advises.

8. Biblical Diversification and God's Will

Biblical diversification is obtained by allocating one's assets into different types of investments that will probably react differently to any particular market condition. For example, during inflationary times, natural resource equities, commodities, and real return bonds generally increase in value, while medium and long-term bonds do poorly.

However, in a period of deflation or disinflation, medium and long-term bonds generally increase in value, while natural resource equities, commodities, and real return bonds do poorly. Further, diversify your assets among several sectors of the economy and different countries; this should reduce the risk and volatility of your total portfolio.

Generally, our portfolios should be well-diversified. Ecclesiastes 11:1–2 advises us to diversify into seven or eight different categories. However, there is no substitute for spending quality time with the Lord in prayer and in his word, sensing his specific will (Isaiah 48:17). There can be unique situations where God directs us not to diversify, but they are rare.

Therefore, *unless* God specifically directs you otherwise (John 10:27), diversify God's investments.

9. Seek God's Direction and Peace

There is no perfect portfolio allocation for all Christians. God's word provides general principles—not specific instructions. That's why there is no substitute for spending quality time in prayer and asking God for his wisdom (James 1:5) and specific direction in investing his money.

Psalm 25:12 says, "Who, then, are those who fear the LORD? He will instruct them in the ways they should choose." If you have no peace in investing in equities because of the risks, perhaps God is directing you to invest in safer categories, such as short-term high-quality bonds or guaranteed investment certificates.

The return on a safe portfolio will be modest. If you just invest in guaranteed investment certificates or short-term high-quality bonds then your return will be less compared to a portfolio that includes a portion in equities. Therefore, you will very likely have to save more money than an investor who assumes reasonable risks within biblical guidelines.

As stewards of God's money, Christians need to invest the money God has entrusted to them based upon the Lord's wisdom (James 1:5) and specific direction.

10. God Discourages Debt

One deception from the world is that smart people use other people's money. In other words, smart people borrow to invest. This is contrary to God's word. In Proverbs 22:7 God warned that the "borrower is slave to the lender."

Of relevance, God never directed anyone in Scripture to borrow money in order for God to meet a need. Our all-powerful God is able to meet every need without the assistance of a lender. Philippians 4:19 states, "My God will meet all your needs according to the riches of his glory in Christ Jesus."

In Deuteronomy 28:1–12, God promised his people that, if they fully obeyed him, they be would lenders, not borrowers. It is not a sin to borrow money; it is a sin to borrow and not repay (Psalm 37:21). However, the pattern throughout Scripture is for God to meet needs without debt. For example, God provided his people with manna and water in the desert for 40 years (Exodus 16).

In summary, God discourages debt; smart people borrow as little as possible and pay it off as soon as possible.

11. The Risks of Investment Loans

Many investment advisers instruct clients to use debt to increase investment returns. People who use debt when investing will generally encounter one of the following problems.

1. When the markets are down, borrowers are forced by the lender to sell at the wrong time. In Proverbs 22:7, God warned that "the borrower is slave to the lender."
2. Psychologically and emotionally, it is much more difficult to survive a bear market (a prolonged period of price declines) when you have borrowed money because debt increases your losses.
3. People lose their original capital and have a debt that takes years to pay.

The pattern throughout Scripture is for God to meet needs without debt. In Matthew 6:31–33, Jesus said:

"Do not worry, saying, 'What shall we eat?' or 'What shall we drink?' or 'What shall we wear?' For the pagans run after all these things, and your heavenly Father knows that you need them. But seek first his kingdom and his righteousness, and all these things will be given to you as well."

In summary, avoid borrowing money to invest; rather, invest whatever cash God provides to you and trust the Lord to meet your needs.

12. Avoid the Temptation to Borrow

It can be tempting to borrow money for investing. When the market goes up, additional returns can be obtained through the use of debt. However, when the market goes down, I've seen many cases where the results were disastrous.

Before you borrow to invest, be sure to ask God to reveal your motives (Proverbs 16:2) by praying as David prayed, "Search me, God, and know my heart; test me and know my anxious thoughts. See if there is any offensive way in me, and lead me in the way everlasting" (Psalm 139:23–24).

Frequently, people use debt because of worldly motives, such as selfishness, lack of contentment, covetousness, and greed—all of which are contrary to God's word. See Philippians 2:3–4, Hebrews 13:5, and Deuteronomy 20:17. Jesus said in Luke 12:15, "Watch out! Be on your guard against all kinds of greed; life does not consist in an abundance of possessions."

On the other hand, saving and investing carefully over a long period of time with the objective of meeting future needs is biblical. "Steady plodding brings prosperity; hasty speculation brings poverty" (Proverbs 21:5, TLB). Proverbs 13:11 states, "Whoever gathers money little by little makes it grow."

In summary, the emphasis in Scripture is to save and invest whatever funds God has provided over a long period of time and to avoid the temptation to borrow money.

13. Understand the Investment

Over the past 44 years, I have had the privilege of working with hundreds of business people. Generally, when they invest in something they understand and are within biblical guidelines, they earn a profit. This is consistent with Proverbs 28:19, which says, "Those who work their land will have abundant food, but those who chase fantasies will have their fill of poverty."

However, when people invest in something they do not understand, frequently they lose money. God warned, "It is dangerous to have zeal without knowledge, and the one who acts hastily makes poor choices" (Proverbs 19:2, NET).

Whether you plan to build a house, an investment portfolio, or a retirement fund, God's word emphasizes the importance of understanding, wisdom, and knowledge. Proverbs 24:3–4 says,

"By wisdom a house is built, and through understanding it is established; through knowledge its rooms are filled with rare and beautiful treasures."

In summary, only invest in things you understand.

14. Seek God's Wisdom for Investments

With respect to investing, on average, only about 15 per cent of all mutual funds beat the relevant index and no human can consistently predict the direction of any market. God is not surprised. As Proverbs 27:1 states, "Do not boast about tomorrow, for you do not know what a day may bring."

The biblical truth is that only God knows the future (Isaiah 46:10), and only he is in control. David praised God, "We adore you as being in control of everything. Riches and honor come from you alone, and you are the ruler of all mankind; your hand controls power and might, and it is at your discretion that men are made great and given strength" (1 Chronicles 29:11–12, TLB).

In other words, as you develop your investment strategy, you need to prayerfully acknowledge that only God knows which investments will do well.

In summary, we must pray and depend on God for his wisdom and direction in investing the money he has entrusted to us.

15. Diversify to Minimize Risk

In Ecclesiastes 11:1–6, God recommended assuming a reasonable amount of risk within an investment portfolio. "Ship your grain across the sea; after many days you may receive a return" was a metaphorical expression in the grain trade that illustrated the potential successful prospects of a business investment.

God instructed the farmer, who is also an investor, "Sow your seed in the morning, and at evening let your hands not be idle, for you do not know which will succeed, whether this or that, or whether both will do equally well" (Ecclesiastes 11:6).

In Proverbs 31, the "wife of noble character" is involved in several equity-type investments. For example, "She considers a field and buys it; out of her earnings she plants a vineyard" (Proverbs 31:16).

In summary, it is biblical to assume some investment risk, but be sure to diversify your investments because we do not know what will happen to any particular market sector or the economy.

16. Assess Your Tolerance for Risk

The risk of any investment portfolio is generally reflected by its allocation between equities and safe investments, such as high-quality bonds or guaranteed investment certificates. The appropriate amount of investment risk will depend upon numerous factors, such as your age, when you will need the money, and your tolerance for risk.

Based on Ecclesiastes 11:4, Christians should not be overly cautious (reflecting a mindset of fear); nor should we be too aggressive (reflecting an attitude of greed—Luke 12:15). Both extremes are outside of God's will.

Under normal economic conditions, and subject to God's specific will, generally a conservative investor should have at least 20 per cent in equities, while an investor with a high tolerance for risk, should not go beyond 70 per cent. The average person may feel comfortable with an allocation of approximately 40 to 50 per cent in equities.

Relying on God's wisdom, assess your tolerance for risk, and invest according to God's principles and specific will.

17. Avoid "Get Rich Quick" Investments

In Proverbs 23:4, God warned, "Do not wear yourself out to get rich; do not trust your own cleverness." Here are the common elements of a typical "get rich quick" investment.

1. It promises an abnormally high rate of return. Logically, if it sounds too good to be true, then it probably is.
2. Generally, the investor has a limited understanding of the investment.
3. The investment requires a quick decision.
4. Debt is used, and the investment is not diversified.

Proverbs 23:5 tells us what often occurs with "get rich quick" investments. "Cast but a glance at riches, and they are gone, for they will surely sprout wings and fly off to the sky like an eagle."

God's approach is different. The emphasis in Scripture is to save and invest a little at a time over a long period—not to try to make a lot of money quickly. "Steady plodding brings prosperity; hasty speculation brings poverty" (Proverbs 21:5, TLB).

18. Avoid Hasty Decisions

When it comes to investing, hasty decisions are usually bad decisions. Proverbs 21:5 says, "The plans of the diligent lead to profit as surely as haste leads to poverty." Before investing, prayerfully consider the following.

1. Ask God to direct you through his Spirit. In John 14:27, Christ promised his peace if we are in his will. A lack of peace could be God directing you not to invest.
2. Ask God to reveal your motives. Proverbs 16:2 makes clear that motives are important to the Lord.

3. Ungodly motives include greed, covetousness, impatience, and pride. Godly motives include generosity, contentment, patience, and humility.

4. Obtain sufficient understanding of the investment (Proverbs 24:3–4).

5. Use godly investment advisers. Psalm 1:1 says, "Blessed is the one who does not walk in step with the wicked."

In summary, don't make hasty decisions, but always take the time to obtain God's direction before investing (Psalm 32:8).

19. Seek Counsel

God admonished us to obtain counsel. Proverbs 15:22 states, "Plans fail for lack of counsel, but with many advisers they succeed." However, be careful to avoid worldly financial counsel.

"Blessed is the man who walks not in the counsel of the ungodly, nor stands in the path of sinners, nor sits in the seat of the scornful; but his delight is in the law of the LORD, and in His law he meditates day and night" (Psalm 1:1–2, NKJV).

And 1 Corinthians 2:14–15 says:

The person without the Spirit does not accept the things that come from the Spirit of God but considers them foolishness, and cannot understand them because they are discerned only through the Spirit. The person with the Spirit makes judgments about all things.

After obtaining godly counsel, it is your responsibility to pray and ask God for his wisdom in weighing that advice. Proverbs 14:15 states, "The simple believe anything, but the prudent give thought to their steps."

Therefore, with respect to any important financial decision, seek godly counsel.

20. Sources of Godly Counsel

Before investing, be sure to obtain godly counsel. Here are four principles for gaining counsel.

1. Prayerfully ask God for his counsel. In 1 Kings 22:5 we read, "Jehoshaphat also said to the king of Israel, 'First seek the counsel of the LORD.'"

2. Review God's investment principles to ensure you are investing within biblical guidelines. For example, use minimal debt—or even better, no debt—as God discouraged the use of debt (Proverbs 22:7). Further, diversify your portfolio (Ecclesiastes 11:2).

3. Seek the advice of two or three godly investment advisers. I would define such a person as a spiritually mature Christian who understands and applies God's investment principles (Psalm 111:10), has a close personal relationship with the Lord (John 15), who has the necessary investment knowledge (Proverbs 24:3–4), and who habitually puts the interests of clients first (Philippians 2:3–4).

4. If you're married, seek the counsel of your spouse. God can give his peace or lack of peace to an objective spouse.

In summary, seek several sources of godly investment counsel as you manage the money God has entrusted to you.

21. Avoid Worldly Motives

Motives are important to God. Proverbs 16:2 says, "All a person's ways seem pure to them, but motives are weighed by the LORD." Worldly motives for investing include the following:

1. Selfishness. Philippians 2:3–4 states, "Do nothing out of selfish ambition or vain conceit. Rather, in humility value others above yourselves, not looking to your own interests but each of you to the interests of the others."
2. Pride. Owning significant wealth can result in pride. But 1 Peter 5:5 is clear, "God opposes the proud but shows favor to the humble."
3. Greed. Jesus said, in Luke 12:15, "Watch out! Be on your guard against all kinds of greed; life does not consist in an abundance of possessions."
4. Trusting in wealth. In the parable of the rich fool (Luke 12:16–21), the man's problem was not that he had significant wealth but rather that he trusted in his wealth, not in God.

In summary, avoid worldly motives for investing *so that God can bless you.*

22. Ensure Your Motives Are Godly

Christians must ensure their motives for investing are godly. Here are some godly examples.

1. Saving and investing in order to meet future needs (1 Timothy 5:8), such as children's education, retirement, car replacement, and purchasing a home—these are all godly motives.
2. Practising good stewardship is also a good motive. If you have given to God everything the Lord has laid upon your heart, then as a good steward you should invest your surplus as the servants did in the parable of the talents (Matthew 25:14–28).

3. Another godly motive for investing is following God's specific will. If God has called you to be in business, then it may be necessary to invest significant amounts in that business.

As Psalm 139:23–24 says, "Search me, God, and know my heart; test me and know my anxious thoughts. See if there is any offensive way in me, and lead me in the way everlasting."

In summary, depend upon God (John 15) to help you develop godly motives for investing.

23. Follow God's Directives, Not Human Tendencies

Our human tendency is to respond to what is happening in the financial markets. Good news provides confidence or triggers greed, which tempts us to buy; bad news generates fear, which results in a desire to sell. So if you rely on your emotions, you will likely buy high and sell low, resulting in losses.

In response to bad news, God gives this directive to the righteous in Psalm 112:7: "They will have no fear of bad news; their hearts are steadfast, trusting in the LORD." Therefore, when you hear bad financial news or if the markets have decreased significantly—before you make any investment decisions, spend quality time with the Lord in prayer. Seek his wisdom (James 1:5) and specific direction (Psalm 32:8).

And at all times, "Trust in the LORD with all your heart, and lean not on your own understanding; in all your ways acknowledge Him, and He shall direct your paths" (Proverbs 3:5–6, NKJV).

24. Avoid Hot Tips and Hasty Decisions

Our human tendency is to make hasty investment decisions in response to hot tips or "once in a lifetime" opportunities. But God recommends planning, diligence, and patience. Proverbs 21:5 states, "The plans of the diligent lead to profit as surely as haste leads to poverty."

Why? Because hasty investment decisions generally result in losses. Always remember, Christ promised to meet our needs if we put him first. In Matthew 6:31–33, Jesus said:

> "Do not worry, saying, 'What shall we eat? or 'What shall we drink?' or 'What shall we wear?' For the pagans run after all these things, and your heavenly Father knows that you need them. But seek first his kingdom and his righteousness, and all these things will be given to you as well."

In summary, avoid hot tips and hasty decisions; diligently plan your investment strategy according to God's principles and will. Proverbs 16:3 assures us, "Commit to the LORD whatever you do, and he will establish your plans."

25. Giving to God's Work Produces Eternal Benefits!

It is easy to become focused on building an investment portfolio, but never forget—financial investments are temporary. The greatest investment of all is giving to God! In Matthew 19:29, Jesus explained, "Everyone who has left houses ... or fields for my sake will receive a hundred times as much and will inherit eternal life."

In Matthew 6:19–21, Jesus admonished us to store up treasures in heaven rather than treasures on earth. One day, we will each be accountable to God. Jesus said, "For the Son of Man is going to come in his Father's glory with his angels, and then he will reward each person according to what they have done" (Matthew 16:27). And in 1 Timothy 6:17–19, we are assured that

Christians who give generously will "lay up treasure for themselves as a firm foundation for the coming age, so that they may take hold of the life that is truly life."

In summary, giving to God's work is an investment with eternal rewards!

26. Keep a Balanced Perspective

Today, we are bombarded with information on investments; it's easy to spend excessive amounts of time and energy on investing, which is not God's will. Proverbs 23:4 says, "Do not wear yourself out to get rich; have the wisdom to show restraint."

It is appropriate for a Christian to spend time learning and applying God's investment principles, but once this has been accomplished, we should trust him for the results. If you prayerfully connect with the Lord (John 15) and follow God's wisdom (James 1:5) and specific direction (Psalm 32:8), then you will have fulfilled your stewardship responsibility. You can leave the results—the return on your investments—to God.

God promised to meet our needs (Matthew 6:31–33) and so we can be content with his provision (1 Timothy 6). Therefore, keep a balanced perspective by investing according to God's direction and trust him for the results (Proverbs 3:5–6).

27. Real-Life Example: The Risks of "Get Rich Quick" Investments

Bob couldn't wait to tell his wife, Judy, about a great investment! Through a friend of a friend, Bob had been given the opportunity to participate in a unique investment that promised abnormally high rates of return. Judy was concerned that she and Bob did not understand the investment and they had no money and would have to borrow all of the funds.

Here are the biblical principles Bob and Judy should consider.

1. Proverbs 19:2 warns against getting involved in something you don't understand.
2. God discouraged debt in Proverbs 22:7, warning, "the borrower is slave to the lender."
3. Any investment that promises an unusually high rate of return means that it's a risky investment (Proverbs 23:4–5).
4. Seek independent godly counsel (Proverbs 15:22; Psalm 1:1–3).
5. Most importantly, prayerfully ask God for his wisdom (James 1:5) and direction (Isaiah 48:17). God will provide his peace (John 14:27) if it is his will.

In summary, if you encounter a proposed investment and it promises an unusually high rate of return, then assess that investment from a biblical perspective as outlined above. This will likely enable you to avoid a lot of losses. Proverbs 28:19–20 states, "Those who work their land will have abundant food, but those who chase fantasies will have their fill of poverty. A faithful person will be richly blessed, but one eager to get rich will not go unpunished."

28. Don't Borrow to Invest

Many people believe the financial deception that smart people use other people's money, In other words, smart people borrow to invest in order to increase their returns.

This is only true if you can predict the future value of an investment—which of course no human can. Proverbs 27:1 warns, "Do not boast about tomorrow, for you do not know what a day may bring."

Further, God warned of the dangers of debt (Proverbs 22:7) and admonished us to save (Proverbs 21:20) for future needs gradually, over a period of time. Proverbs 13:11 says, "Dishonest money dwindles away, but whoever gathers money little by little makes it grow."

Not surprisingly—to me, anyhow—in Deuteronomy 28:12, God promised his people that if they fully obeyed him, they would not have to borrow.

In summary, God's desire is for us to save gradually in order to meet future needs and not to borrow to invest.

29. Good Debt Versus Bad Debt

Some people believe that there is good debt and bad debt. Generally speaking, "good debt" would be money borrowed for things like education or a house. "Bad debt" would be money borrowed for unnecessary purchases, often using credit cards.

There is certainly a difference between a wise and foolish use of money, but this distinction between "good debt" and "bad debt" is not provided in Scripture. All references about borrowing in the Bible are negative; God discouraged debt (Proverbs 22:7). The pattern throughout Scripture is for God to meet needs with no debt.

Since He is the King of kings and Lord of lords, God can meet needs without the assistance of a lender. For example, God provided food and water provided to the Israelites during the 40 years in the desert (Exodus 16:35). In Matthew 6:31–33, Jesus promised to meet our needs if we put him first. And in Philippians 4:19, Paul said, "My God will meet all your needs."

In summary, God discourages debt and instructs us to trust him to meet our needs.

To learn more about God's investment principles, watch the three half-hour videos at www.coplandfinancialministries.org. We have numerous other resources there, most of which are free. You can also follow @biblefinance on Facebook, Instagram, and Twitter.

BIBLICALLY BASED ESTATE PLANNING

1. Biblical and Stewardship Estate Planning

Let's discuss estate planning.

1. Who owns your assets? Psalm 24:1 answers, "The earth is the LORD's, and everything in it, the world, and all who live in it."
2. Who owns your money? "'The silver is mine and the gold is mine,' declares the LORD Almighty" (Haggai 2:8).
3. Is there anything that God does not own? God said to Job, "Everything under heaven belongs to me" (Job 41:11).

Since God owns everything, we are stewards of the assets God has entrusted to us. Therefore, we must look to the owner—that is, God—for how we plan our estates.

God's word has incredible financial wisdom for all aspects of life, including estate planning. However, most Christians are not aware of what the Bible says about estate planning. As a result, they plan their estates and prepare their wills without prayer and without God's wisdom from his word.

In summary, plan your estate by seeking God's wisdom through prayer and studying the numerous Scriptures that apply to estate planning.

2. Allocate Assets According to God's Will

Unfortunately, most Christians do not prayerfully search God's word for his wisdom in planning their estate. For example, many parents believe that in their will, they must allocate their assets equally among their children *regardless* of how they manage money.

This thinking is not consistent with Scripture. In the parable of the talents, the master (who is God) entrusted more to those servants who were faithful in managing money, while he took away what the unfaithful servant had (Matthew 25:14–30).

Therefore, as good stewards of God's assets (Haggai 2:8), when you plan your estate, be sure to consider the money management habits of your children. However, if a child who mismanages money has legitimate needs he or she cannot provide for, then consider using a trust or an annuity to ensure that the child's needs are met and the money is not squandered. Also, it may be necessary to allocate more to a child with a disability (1 Timothy 5:8).

In summary, plan your estate and allocate assets according to God's will (Psalm 25:12). Be sure to take into consideration the money management habits of your children and their specific needs.

3. Consider Giving Prior to Death

Although it is biblical to save (Luke 14:28–30) for future needs such as retirement, sometimes even Christians accumulate significantly more than necessary. In the parable of the rich fool (Luke 12:16–21), Christ warned against hoarding.

Therefore, in the process of estate planning, project your future needs and prayerfully consider giving the surplus while you are living. Why?

1. Assets given pursuant to your will require no personal sacrifice because as Paul said, "We brought nothing into the world, and we can take nothing out of it" (1 Timothy 6:7).

2. God will bless generous givers. In Luke 6:38, Jesus said, "Give, and it will be given to you."

3. God promises eternal rewards to those who give generously while on earth. 1 Timothy 6:18–19 says, "Command them to do good, to be rich in good deeds, and to be generous and willing to share. In this way they will lay up treasure for themselves as a firm foundation for the coming age."

In summary, project for future family needs and give God the surplus while you are living.

4. Seek Godly Counsel in Estate Planning

In the process of planning your estate, be sure to seek godly counsel. As 1 Corinthians 2:14–15 says:

The person without the Spirit does not accept the things that come from the Spirit of God but considers them foolishness, and cannot understand them because they are discerned only through the Spirit. The person with the Spirit makes judgments about all things, but such a person is not subject to merely human judgments.

Only a spiritually mature Christian will provide biblically based financial advice. For example, a non-believer will not understand a Christian's desire to give generously to God's work. This is because the Christian has an eternal perspective, wanting to build up "treasures in heaven," while the non-believer has a temporal perspective, wanting to build up "treasures on earth" (Matthew 6:19–21).

Weigh all advice received against God's word because unfortunately, some Christians give financial advice that is contrary to biblical principles.

In summary, in the process of planning your estate, obtain counsel from godly advisers, review God's word on estate planning, and above all, prayerfully "seek the counsel of the LORD" (1 Kings 22:5).

5. Transfer Wisdom Before Assets

With respect to estate planning, teach all your heirs God's financial wisdom before transferring assets. "Why is there money in the hand of a fool to buy wisdom, When he has no sense?" (Proverbs 17:16, NASB). In Luke 16:10, Jesus said, "Whoever can be trusted with very little can also be trusted with much, and whoever is dishonest with very little will also be dishonest with much."

In other words, if your children have not been faithful stewards in managing their money, they will not be faithful in managing your money after you die. And if your children have been mismanaging money, don't bail them out. Bailing them out enables them to continue with their worldly management of money and they will not learn from their mistakes.

In conclusion, teach your children God's way of managing money before you transfer assets. Proverbs 22:6 says, "Start children off on the way they should go, and even when they are old they will not turn from it."

6. Prayerfully Seek God's Wisdom and Direction

In 1 Chronicles, King David acknowledged God's ownership of all his assets. Here's what he said,

> "Yours is the mighty power and glory and victory and majesty. Everything in the heavens and earth is yours, O Lord, and this is your kingdom. We adore you as being

in control of everything. Riches and honor come from you alone, and you are the ruler of all mankind; your hand controls power and might, and it is at your discretion that men are made great and given strength." (1 Chronicles 29:11–12, TLB)

Similarly today, we need to acknowledge God's ownership of our assets and prayerfully seek his wisdom and direction in estate planning. James 1:5 says, "If any of you lacks wisdom, you should ask God, who gives generously to all without finding fault, and it will be given to you." And in Psalm 32:8, God promised, "I will instruct you and teach you in the way you should go; I will counsel you with my loving eye on you."

In summary, be sure to spend quality time with the Lord in prayer, reading his word, and asking God for his wisdom and specific direction in planning your estate.

7. A Will Is Your Final Stewardship Decision

Many surveys show that a very small percentage of Christians leave anything in their will to God's work. Unfortunately, most Christians do not understand that their will is their final stewardship decision—and probably the most important legal document they will ever sign. The reason for its importance is that your will governs all of your assets after you die. Other legal documents, such as the purchase of a house or a car, only govern those specific assets.

When you do your estate plan and prepare your will, be sure to allocate a generous portion to God's work. In Matthew 16:27, Jesus said, "For the Son of Man is going to come in his Father's glory with his angels, and then he will reward each person according to what they have done."

Scripture is clear that there will be rewards in heaven for those Christians who do some biblically based estate planning.

However, most Christians are not aware that there are many Scripture verses that apply to estate planning. Of interest, I have eight half-hour videos that teach the biblical principles with respect to estate planning.

You can find them at www.coplandfinancialministries.org.

8. Consider Trust and Annuities

When you plan your estate and have your will prepared, consider utilizing a trust or an annuity—particularly for beneficiaries who mismanage money. This ensures that they do not squander your hard-earned money after you die.

A trust is a legal arrangement generally created pursuant to one's will where the funds designated for a specific beneficiary are not distributed to that person immediately. Rather, the trustee decides when and how the funds should be used.

Another option is to provide instructions in your will for the executor to purchase a life annuity for a beneficiary who mismanages money. Appoint a guardian in your will for children who are under 18 years of age. I recommend that you have your will prepared by an experienced lawyer as it is such an important document.

Remember, your will is your final stewardship decision as it will govern all of your assets after you die; having a proper will is consistent with good biblical stewardship.

9. Minimize Disputes After You Die

Unfortunately, there often disputes among siblings, and sometimes lawsuits, after their parents have died. You and your spouse (if you're married) can minimize the risk of these disputes by planning your estate and will carefully. Here are some ideas.

Communicate to your heirs your decisions regarding the allocation of your assets at a high level. Surprises after your death often give rise to disputes among siblings. Such communication would include that you are allocating a portion to the Lord's work. If God has directed you to do so, it should also include that you are allocating more to one child versus another child. Again, just provide the big-picture overview. Do not provide details; you also do not have to share with your kids the total value of your assets.

If the Lord leads, consider giving some of your assets to your kids before you die. But ensure that you have sufficient for your retirement, healthcare costs, and any other costs. If you have loaned money to one of your kids, make it clear in your will as to whether it is a forgivable loan or if that child's share of the estate should be reduced accordingly.

I've seen many cases where a parent has loaned money to one child, and after the parent dies, that child believes it was a forgivable loan and should not impact their allocation from their parents' estate. However, the other siblings argue that the amount of the loan should be deducted from the debtor's pro rata share, which would result in more being allocated to them.

In summary, do everything you can to plan your estate, and prepare your will in order to minimize disputes among your kids and any other heirs after you have died.

10. Be Careful of Leaving Large Estates to Your Kids

If you have been blessed by God financially, be careful how you leave a significant estate to your children after you die. Receiving large estates can enable laziness, selfishness, lack of perseverance, and trust in wealth.

A beneficiary's current management of money reveals how they will likely use any inheritance (Luke 16:10). Do not feel you have to leave equal amounts to each child. In the parable of the talents, God gave five talents to one servant, two talents to another servant, and one talent to a third (Matthew 25:15).

Consider the unique circumstances of each child. One child may have greater legitimate needs, another could be in full-time ministry, another could manage money God's way, while another child may squander money. Ask God to reveal to you in prayer, through his word and biblical counsel, where he wants you to allocate his assets. Remember, it's not your kids' money; it is not even your money. It's all God's money. Therefore, you need to do God's will (Luke 22:42) in allocating the assets the Lord has entrusted to you.

11. Discerning God's Will

In doing estate planning, sometimes there are complicated circumstances. For example, one of your kids may squander money, another could be disabled and have significant financial needs, and another could be in full-time ministry. The Bible provides biblical guidelines; however, there can be several options within the guidelines, so each Christian needs to discern what God wants them to do. Here are some suggestions.

Acknowledge that you are a steward of God's resources (Haggai 2:8); pray and ask God for his wisdom and his direction (James 1:5); review the Scriptures that apply to estate planning (Psalm 119:105); and obtain biblical counsel.

Be careful of external pressure (including from your kids), and be sure to please God rather than people (1 Thessalonians 2:4). Ensure that you have enough to live on for the rest of your life. If you do, consider giving more to the Lord's work, and possibly to your kids who have needs, while you are alive. As the saying goes, consider "doing your giving while you are living so you know where it's going."

Look for consistent direction from more than one source—Scripture, counsel, prayer, and God's peace (John 14:27)—before making a final decision.

12. What About Your Parents' Estate Planning?

Have your parents developed a biblically based estate plan? Many adult kids will be a beneficiary and/or executor of their parents' estate. When no estate planning is done, often there are problems, including disputes among family members and excessive tax liabilities. If your parents have not developed a biblically based estate plan, here are some suggestions.

If they are not Christians, explain some of the practical benefits of estate planning, such as the following.

1. Estate planning can save significant taxes (Matthew 22:21).
2. The risks of disputes among their children can be substantially reduced.
3. Many legal complexities will be avoided.
4. The work for the executor can be substantially reduced.

If they are Christians, encourage them to learn what the Bible says on estate planning. Remind them that their wills are their final stewardship decision and thus very important from an eternal perspective. Jesus said, "For the Son of Man is going to come in his Father's glory with his angels, and then he will reward each person according to what they have done" (Matthew 16:27).

13. Case Study: Jack and Jill

Jack and Jill are elderly, and they have four children with the following circumstances. Jake and his wife earn substantial salaries, but they spend excessively and have significant debts. Roger has disabilities and is unemployable. Caleb and his wife serve as full-time missionaries in a developing country, but they are underfunded. Ron and his wife manage money in God's way, have no debt, and give generously to God's work.

Most people would allocate their assets equally among their kids, regardless of their unique circumstances. However, after considerable prayer, study of God's word, and biblical counsel, Jack and Jill decide to allocate more to Roger in order to meet his needs (1 Timothy 5:8).

Their next priority is Caleb and his wife, to support their underfunded full-time missionary work. After that, they will allocate a reasonable amount to Ron because he has practised biblical stewardship. As for Jake who squanders money, it is biblical to allocate less to him based upon the parable of the talents (Matthew 25:14–30).

In summary, consider the unique circumstances of each child's situation as you prayerfully make your estate planning decisions.

14. Estate Planning Summary

Here's a summary of the biblical principles on estate planning.

1. You are a steward; God is the owner!
2. The wise Christian studies the many Scriptures that apply to estate planning in order to obtain God's wisdom (James 1:5) and specific direction (Psalm 32:8).
3. It is biblical to leave more to those who have managed money in God's way as opposed to those who have squandered money (Matthew 25:14–30).

4. If you have a child who is disabled, you should provide for their needs (1 Timothy 5:8), and use a trust if necessary.
5. Transfer wisdom before you transfer wealth to your kids (Proverbs 22:6).
6. Do some estate tax planning so the government gets less and your kids receive more (Matthew 22:21).
7. If you have more than you need to live on for the rest of your life, do some additional giving while you're alive.
8. Finally, allocate a portion to the Lord's work pursuant to your will; it saves tax and God will bless you in eternity! (Matthew 16:27).

To learn more about biblically based estate planning, be sure to check out our eight half-hour videos and other resources on our website, www.coplandfinancialministries.org. If you have any questions, please send us an email at info@biblefinance.org. You can also follow @biblefinance on Facebook, Instagram, and Twitter.

XVII.
GOD'S FINANCIAL WISDOM FOR YOUNG PEOPLE

1. A Common Real-Life Example

Let me share with you a story I've seen hundreds of times. A young man and woman attend university or college. They have not saved money for their education costs, including tuition fees, books, and accommodation. And since credit is so readily available, they both obtain student loans and lines of credit, and credit cards. As a result, they accumulate a lot of debt.

This young couple meets each other, falls in love, and gets married. They both get full-time jobs and purchase cars with zero per cent financing. Not long after, they purchase a home. Because they have no savings, they borrow the down payment from their parents and take on a large mortgage.

Their student loans, credit cards, car loans, and big mortgage accumulate to a huge amount. As a result, they encounter significant financial problems. At this point, they ask each other, "How did we ever get into this financial mess?" Unfortunately, this couple has unknowingly been violating many biblical financial principles, and they are now suffering the consequences.

2. Dealing With Excessive Debt

If you have accumulated a lot of debt, here's what you should do:

1. Learn what God's word says about finances. Unfortunately, most Christians have limited knowledge of what the Bible says about finances and end up suffering the consequences because they have unknowingly violated God's principles.

2. Develop and implement a monthly budget or cash flow plan to ensure you are spending less than you earn so you have a surplus to pay down debt. Generally, pay off your credit cards first.
3. Learn to be content with less. In Philippians 4:11–13, Paul said:

I have learned to be content whatever the circumstances. I know what it is to be in need, and I know what it is to have plenty. I have learned the secret of being content in any and every situation, whether well fed or hungry, whether living in plenty or in want. I can do all this through him who gives me strength.

We know that Paul was a committed Christian, and even he had to learn to be content.

In summary, learn to be content by focusing on your relationship with Jesus Christ and things of eternal value. As a result, temporal things such as money will become less important.

3. Debt Restricts Your Future Options

Today, most young people accumulate too much debt during their post-secondary education and several years thereafter. Student loans, student lines of credit, and credit cards create a phenomenal temptation to borrow and buy.

Since 1982, I've counselled thousands of young people, and often I will ask them to review their expenditures over the previous several years. This generally reveals that they spent a lot of money on wants and desires as opposed to needs. In other words, most of the debt was unnecessary.

Unfortunately, most young people do not realize that debt accumulation can restrict their future options. For example, they may not be able to pay for a postgraduate degree, go into full-time ministry, or obtain mortgage financing when they want to buy their first home. Unintentionally, they became "a slave to the lender" (Proverbs 22:7) as the accumulated debt restricts their future options.

In summary, be very careful how much debt you take on, make sure you have a plan to pay it back, and understand that it can very easily restrict your future options.

4. Managing Money God's Way Brings Benefits

Unlike most university and college students, Caleb learned what God's word said about finances. He saw that God discouraged borrowing (Proverbs 22:7) and that the Lord promised to meet our needs but not necessarily our wants and desires (Matthew 6:31–33).

During high school and university, Caleb followed Christ's admonition in the parable of the tower (Luke 14:28–30) to save for future needs, by estimating all future university-related costs, including tuition fees, books, and accommodations. He then developed annual budgets to meet those needs.

Caleb worked diligently full-time during the summers and part-time during the school years, earning sufficient income so that when he graduated from university, he had no debt! Praise God!

Unlike most university graduates, Caleb followed biblical financial principles, resulting in no debt. As a result, he has the option to obtain further education, including Bible school. Caleb is not experiencing financial stress; further, he and his fiancée can afford to get married next year because she has also learned and applied biblical principles for managing money.

5. Excessive Debt Can Destroy Your Marriage Relationship

Peter and Laura met at university and fell in love. A few years later, they were married. Unfortunately, Peter and Laura had no idea that the accumulation of significant debt—starting during their university years—would result in serious long-term problems. These problems included being turned down on a mortgage when they went to purchase their first home and undergoing tremendous financial stress that was destroying their relationship.

Whenever the topic of money came up, Peter and Laura inevitably ended up arguing about their finances and how to deal with their debts. In my experience, most couples say finances are the most frequent topic they argue about. Of interest, there is generally enough money in these situations. The issue is that either one or both spouses are unknowingly violating biblical financial principles by spending more than they are earning, accumulating debt, and later suffering the consequences.

If you find that you and your spouse are in this situation, you may ask, *What's the solution?* The answer is that both husbands and wives need to learn to manage money according to God's financial principles.

6. Planning and Saving for Future Needs

Most young people do not save in advance for their post-secondary education. Instead, they spend all their money and accumulate significant debt when they attend university or college. This is not God's will. "The wise man saves for the future, but the foolish man spends whatever he gets" (Proverbs 21:20, TLB).

It is biblical and much better for you to have a full-time job in the summer and a part-time job while you are going to school so you can pay for as many of your expenses as possible. This is biblical and wiser than accumulating debt on credit cards, student lines of credit, and student loans.

In the parable of the tower (Luke 14:28–30), Christ admonished us to plan ahead. The most practical way to do that is to develop a budget/spending plan and save in advance for future costs, such as tuition fees, books, and accommodation, so you will have the necessary funds. As a result, you will not be forced into debt. Long-term, you will be much better off!

7. Godly Versus Worldly Attitudes Toward Money

Proverbs 16:2 says, "All a person's ways seem pure to them, but motives are weighed by the LORD." In other words, your motives for buying something are very important to God. Unfortunately, because of worldly motives, such as covetousness and selfishness, many young people buy things they do not need—often on credit—and thus accumulate debt.

The corresponding godly motive is contentment. In 1 Timothy 6:6–8, Paul said, "Godliness with contentment is great gain. For we brought nothing into the world, and we can take nothing out of it. But if we have food and clothing, we will be content with that." And in Luke 3:14, John the Baptist said, "Be content with your pay."

In summary, God wants us to be content with his provision and learn to live within the income the Lord has provided. Therefore, do not use credit cards or student loans that enable you to live beyond your means.

8. We Are Stewards of God's Money

Because many young people have limited income, they often feel they do not have to be concerned about being a good steward of what God has entrusted to them. This is not true!

What do these verses say about the ownership of money and material things? Psalm 24:1 says, "The earth is the LORD's, and everything in it." Haggai 2:8 says: "'The silver is mine and the gold is mine,' declares the LORD Almighty."

Since silver and gold were used as money when this Scripture was written, God is saying that all money is his. Therefore, we are stewards or managers of the money he has entrusted to us. God is the owner!

As stewards, we need to look to God for how we should manage his resources. With over 2,300 references in the Bible to money and material things, God has much instruction for us.

9. Our Stewardship Responsibilities

For young, middle-aged, and older people, I believe that Christian stewardship is fundamentally the same. Here's my definition of Christian stewardship:

1. Acknowledge in your heart and mind that God owns everything (Psalm 24:1).
2. Use money and material things in accordance with God's principles and specific will (Luke 22:42).

In order to accomplish this, you should:

3. Habitually spend quality time with the Lord in prayer, asking God for wisdom in managing money (James 1:5).
4. Study and meditate on God's word about finances. Joshua 1:8 says, "Keep this Book of the Law always on your lips; meditate on it day and night, so that you may be careful to do everything written in it. Then you will be prosperous and successful."
5. Manage money according to God's specific will, and trust him to direct you. "Trust in the LORD with all your

heart, and lean not on your own understanding; in all your ways acknowledge Him, and He shall direct your paths" (Proverbs 3:5–6, NKJV).

In summary, acknowledge in your heart and mind that you are a steward of God's resources, and use his money according to God's principles and his specific will.

10. Contentment Is the Antidote to Many Worldly Attitudes

Many young people struggle with worldly attitudes toward money and material things, including covetousness, selfishness, and greed. As a result, they spend money unnecessarily on things like designer clothes, vacations, and expensive smartphones. This can lead to accumulating debt and later suffering the consequences.

The antidote to these worldly desires is to learn contentment. In Philippians 4:11–13, Paul said:

I have learned to be content whatever the circumstances. I know what it is to be in need, and I know what it is to have plenty. I have learned the secret of being content in any and every situation, whether well fed or hungry, whether living in plenty or in want. I can do all this through him who gives me strength.

Paul's secret to learning contentment was to focus on his personal relationship with Jesus Christ and things of eternal value, such as the salvation of people. In other words, Paul had an eternal perspective rather than a temporal perspective. When you have an eternal perspective, money and material things will become much less important to you, and you will learn contentment.

If you would like to learn more about God's financial wisdom for young people, be sure to watch the eight half-hour videos on this topic and check out the other resources on our website www.coplandfinancialministries.org. You can also follow @biblefinance on Facebook, Instagram, and Twitter.

XVIII.
BUSINESS

1. We Are Stewards of God's Business

Are you a business owner? If yes, then consider King David's words:

> "Everything in the heavens and earth is yours, O Lord, and this is your kingdom. We adore you as being in control of everything. Riches and honor come from you alone, and you are the ruler of all mankind; your hand controls power and might, and it is at your discretion that men are made great and given strength." (1 Chronicles 29:11–12, TLB)

Since the absolute truth is that God owns everything, then logically, we are stewards of the business he has entrusted to us. God is the owner! As stewards, we need to look to the owner for how we should manage his business. With over 2,300 references in the Bible to money, God has much instruction for us.

In summary, acknowledge God's ownership of your business. Learn and apply God's business principles so you can fulfill your stewardship responsibilities.

2. Biblical Stewardship

Business owners should consider the following Scripture verses.

In Haggai 2:8, God said, "'The silver is mine and the gold is mine,' declares the Lord Almighty." Since silver and gold were used as money at that time, God is saying that all money is his.

In Psalm 50:7, 10–12, God reminded his people:

"Listen, my people, and I will speak; I will testify against you, Israel: I am God, your God … For every animal of the forest is mine, and the cattle on a thousand hills. I know every bird in the mountains, and the insects in the fields are mine. If I were hungry I would not tell you, for the world is mine, and all that is in it."

Remember that at the time this Scripture was written, most people were farmers, and cattle would be analogous to business inventory or equipment. So God is saying to business owners that he owns all your business assets; you are a steward of the business the Lord has entrusted to you.

In summary, as God's stewards, we must utilize the resources of our businesses according to his principles and specific will.

3. Our Stewardship Responsibilities

Business owners should consider their stewardship responsibilities. Here's my definition of those responsibilities.

Christian stewardship is acknowledging in heart and mind that God owns everything—including the business he has entrusted to you. It also means using your personal and corporate funds and all your business assets in accordance with God's principles and his specific will.

In order to be a good steward of "God's business," we should habitually spend quality time with the Lord in prayer, asking for his wisdom (James 1:5) and his direction (Psalm 25:12). Further, we should meditate on key Scriptures that deal with business finances. Joshua 1:8 states, "Keep this Book of the Law always on your lips; meditate on it day and night, so that you may be careful to do everything written in it. Then you will be prosperous and successful."

God is not guaranteeing that you're going to be super successful. But the Lord does promise (Matthew 6:31–33) that he will meet your personal and business needs as you put him first—in other words, as you manage your business and personal finances according to biblical financial principles.

In summary, manage all aspects of your business according to God's way and trust him to meet your needs. "Trust in the LORD with all your heart, and lean not on your own understanding; in all your ways acknowledge Him, and He shall direct your paths" (Proverbs 3:5–6, NKJV).

4. A Common Example of Bad Business Stewardship

Here is a common example of bad business stewardship. Mark owns and manages his own business. He spends all the profits and has accumulated significant corporate debt in order to expand his business. Mark does not follow a budget either corporately or personally. Meeting payroll and paying bills on time is generally a struggle, and he regularly pays suppliers late.

Even though Mark is a Christian, without realizing it, he has violated many biblical financial principles that apply to managing one's business. For example, God discouraged debt and warned of its dangers (Proverbs 22:7). Yet Mark is using debt quite freely and is now suffering the consequences. Further, since he does not pay his suppliers on time, he is not a light into a world of darkness (Matthew 5:14–16). Therefore, he is a bad testimony as a Christian to his suppliers.

In the parable of the tower (Luke 14:28–30), Christ admonished us to plan ahead. Hence, a business owner should develop a corporate budget and cash flow plan to ensure that all bills are paid on time and provide working capital for future growth. Very few business owners do this.

Mark needs to learn and apply God's financial principles for managing the business God has entrusted to him. James 1:22 states: "Do not merely listen to the word, and so deceive yourselves. Do what it says."

5. A Common Example of Biblical Business Stewardship

Here is an example of biblical business stewardship. Ron owns and manages a business. He has studied God's financial principles that apply to business and personal money management. Ron has followed biblical financial principles in managing his business.

For example, Ron develops and implements a corporate budget and cash flow plan each year to ensure there are sufficient funds to meet all financial obligations, as well as a cushion of cash to meet unexpected expenditures so that his company is prepared for recessionary times.

Proverbs 21:5 says, "The plans of the diligent lead to profit as surely as haste leads to poverty." In other words, corporate financial planning is biblical, and if it's done properly, in conjunction with discerning God's specific will (Psalm 32:8), almost without exception your business will be profitable.

In addition, Proverbs 21:20 says: "The wise store up choice food and olive oil, but fools gulp theirs down." Unfortunately, most business people fall into the foolish category by spending all of their income and having no cushion of cash to fall back on during difficult times. As a result, they will eventually suffer the consequences.

However, in Ron's case, he applied biblical financial principles and followed God's will. Thus, by age 45, Ron paid off all corporate and personal debts, and he and his wife are experiencing God's peace in the area of finances (John 14:27).

6. Give God the Firstfruits of Your Business

Linda owns and manages a business. God has blessed her business with significant profits. Although a friend encouraged Linda to give generously to God's work, Linda and her company give very little.

Linda comments that she has worked hard and should be able to enjoy a big salary. Besides, she plans to reinvest all the remaining profits to grow the business so that at a later date, she can give even more to the Lord's work. Unfortunately, Linda has not made giving to God's work a priority. Proverbs 3:9 says, "Honor the Lord with your wealth, with the firstfruits of all your crops."

Linda needs to understand that she is a steward (1 Corinthians 4:2) of the business God has entrusted to her. If Linda is not faithful to the Lord, as demonstrated in the parable of the talents (Matthew 25), God may take away her successful business and give it to another Christian who acknowledges God's ownership and gives generously to God's work.

7. Business Giving

If you own and manage a business, let me encourage you to give generously to God's work. Give not only with respect to the salaries you take from your company but also a portion of the profits that are left in the corporation. In Matthew 6:19–21, Jesus said:

> "Do not store up for yourselves treasures on earth, where moths and vermin destroy, and where thieves break in and steal. But store up for yourselves treasures in heaven, where moths and vermin do not destroy, and where thieves do not break in and steal. For where your treasure is, there your heart will be also."

I understand your challenge. It is very easy to become focused on building a business; but remember, your business is temporary. As Paul said, "We brought nothing into the world, and we can take nothing out of it" (1 Timothy 6:7).

So as God blesses your business, avoid hoarding (Luke 12:15), and give generously to God's work. Jesus said, "It is more blessed to give than to receive" (Acts 20:35).

8. Has God Blessed Your Business?

Has God blessed your business? If yes, I would encourage you to consider what Paul said in 1 Timothy 6:17–19:

> Command those who are rich in this present world not to be arrogant nor to put their hope in wealth, which is so uncertain, but to put their hope in God, who richly provides us with everything for our enjoyment. Command them to do good, to be rich in good deeds, and to be generous and willing to share. In this way they will lay up treasure for themselves as a firm foundation for the coming age.

As you can see, giving to God's work enables you to convert a temporal asset, such as money, into something of eternal value! And in Matthew 16:27, Jesus said, "The Son of Man is going to come in his Father's glory with his angels, and then he will reward each person according to what they have done."

As God blesses your business, I encourage you to raise your standard of giving, not your standard of living. Giving to God's work can be done in many ways. You can give money to your local church and parachurch organizations. You can give of your time. You can give the resources of your business, such as using some of your business facilities or staff for ministry purposes. Over the years, I've seen lots of creative ways that business people have used the resources of their businesses to expand God's kingdom.

9. If It Is the Lord's Will, We Will Do This or That

Prayerfully consider this biblical business principle in James 4:13–15:

> Now listen, you who say, "Today or tomorrow we will go to this or that city, spend a year there, carry on business and make money." Why, you do not even know what will happen tomorrow. What is your life? You are a mist that appears for a little while and then vanishes. Instead, you ought to say, "If it is the Lord's will, we will live and do this or that."

Since only God knows the future (Isaiah 46:10) and only the Lord is in control (Psalm 103:19), wise Christian business owners pray and discern God's specific will before making any major financial decision. Unfortunately, most Christians make business decisions without consulting the Lord; later, they ask God to bless their decisions, or they ask him to bail them out of the financial mess they have gotten themselves into.

In summary, God wants us to discern his specific will (Luke 22:42) before making any major business financial decisions.

10. Discerning God's Will for Your Business

If you own and manage your own business, I would encourage you to consider the following steps to discern God's specific will before making any important business decision.

1. Spent quality time with the Lord in prayer, asking for his wisdom (James 1:5) and specific direction (Psalm 32:8).

2. Study God's word, asking the Lord to highlight specific verses to give you clear direction (Psalm 119:105).

3. Be sure to obtain godly counsel from a committed Christian business owner (1 Corinthians 2:14–15) before proceeding.

I've seen business owners pray about expanding their business. After reading numerous Scripture passages that apply to business, God will often highlight a key verse through his Spirit.

One such verse might be Psalm 37:7, which says, "Be still before the LORD and wait patiently for him." Another Scripture could be Isaiah 64:4, which says that God "acts on behalf of those who wait for him."

In other words, their idea could be a good one, but the timing is not right. Or God could highlight a verse that encourages them to move ahead.

11. Hire Employees of High-Quality Character

Are you working too many hours as a business owner? One solution is to hire employees and delegate work to them. Jethro advised Moses to do this in Exodus 18. However, be sure to hire employees of the highest-quality godly character—people who fear God, who are trustworthy and honest (Exodus 18:21).

Most employers just hire the person with the most experience and training. Of course, that is important, but if that employee has an attitude or character problem, then it's not going to work out long-term.

In managing my own business since 1982, I have hired based upon character first, and it has really paid off. If someone doesn't have the experience or training, we can provide that for them; however, if they have a character issue, you or I cannot change that.

In summary, focus on character and hire godly employees; train them and delegate work to them so you can live a balanced lifestyle.

12. Availability of Financing

Are you considering expanding your business? Generally, expanding one's business is appropriate. However, in the last four decades, I have seen many people who were planning to expand their business interpret the availability of the financing as God opening the door for them to go ahead.

It's important to understand that the availability of financing may be God directing you to proceed with the business expansion; however, it could also be Satan tempting you to get into debt. Satan wants Christians to be servants to the lender (Proverbs 22:7). But of course, we are here on earth to serve God and not the bank.

The Bible discourages debt and encourages saving for future needs. Proverbs 21:20 says: "The wise store up choice food and olive oil, but fools gulp theirs down."

In conclusion, it is often better to save for future expansion rather than borrowing each time, which is the world's perspective.

13. Serve God, Not Money

In Matthew 6:24, Jesus said, "No one can serve two masters. Either you will hate the one and love the other, or you will be devoted to the one and despise the other. You cannot serve both God and money."

For everyone, including business owners, it is easy to unintentionally serve money rather than God. Here are some examples of serving money. You are working so many hours that your life is out of balance and you are not spending quality time with the Lord in prayer each day. If you have a family or are in ministry, your extra work hours could mean you are not spending quality time with your spouse and kids or serving in ministry.

You may say you put God first. However, where you spend your time and money reveals your true priorities. Jesus said, "For where your treasure is, there your heart will be also" (Matthew 6:21).

What is the solution? It is to follow the greatest commandment. As Jesus said, "Love the Lord your God with all your heart and with all your soul and with all your mind" (Matthew 22:37).

As a Christian business owner or manager, you need to set your priorities in accordance with biblical principles. That is, put God first, your spouse and your kids second, and then your business and ministry.

14. Your Relationship With God Should Be Your Highest Priority

Managing one's own business often requires a lot of time and effort. Unfortunately, this means many business owners and managers neglect their relationship with the Lord. If you do not develop and maintain a close relationship with Jesus Christ, you will miss out on his wisdom and related blessings. Isaiah 48:17 says, "I am the LORD your God, who teaches you what is best for you, who directs you in the way you should go."

However, when we put God first, he will meet our needs. In Matthew 6:31–33, Jesus said:

> "Do not worry, saying, 'What shall we eat? or 'What shall we drink?' or 'What shall we wear?' For the pagans run after all these things, and your heavenly Father knows that you need them. But seek first his kingdom and his

righteousness, and all these things will be given to you as well."

So if you put God first when managing your business and personal life, then God has promised to provide for the needs of your business. This includes customer sales, positive cash flow, key employees, and what's needed with respect to office or industrial space to operate your business.

Therefore, before making any important business decision, be sure to spend quality time with the Lord in prayer, seeking his counsel and wisdom. As Jehoshaphat said to the king of Israel, "First seek the counsel of the Lord" (1 Kings 22:5).

15. God Has a Plan for Your Business!
In Jeremiah 29:11–13, God said:

> "For I know the plans I have for you," declares the LORD, "plans to prosper you and not to harm you, plans to give you hope and a future. Then you will call on me and come and pray to me, and I will listen to you. You will seek me and find me when you seek me with all your heart."

In other words, God has a plan for you and for your business as well. Remember, the best business decision today depends on future events. Since only God knows the future (John 16:13) and since only he is in control (Psalm 103:19), the wise Christian business owner prayerfully seeks God's wisdom and direction to discern the Lord's specific will.

Discerning and following God's will is always the best decision! How do you do this? Pray and ask God for his wisdom, study God's word as it applies to business, and obtain godly counsel. Finally, ask God to speak to you through his word and through his Spirit (Hebrews 4:12).

16. Use Your Business for Ministry!

Christian business owners should prayerfully consider using their business resources for ministry. Not only should you give generously to God's work, but also be creative in utilizing the business resources God has entrusted to you for eternal purposes! Here are a few examples.

1. Manage your company with total integrity so that you will be a light into a world of darkness (Matthew 5:14–16).
2. Witness to your clients, suppliers, and employees as God opens doors (Matthew 10:32). Do this with "gentleness and respect," as Peter instructed us (1 Peter 3:15).
3. Use office space for ministry purposes, such as a discipleship program after hours.
4. Help employees financially (beyond their regular salary) when you see a significant need.
5. Pray, seek biblical counsel, and ask God to show you how you can use his business for his glory.

In Ephesians 5:15–17, Paul said, "Be very careful, then, how you live—not as unwise but as wise, making the most of every opportunity, because the days are evil. Therefore do not be foolish, but understand what the Lord's will is."

Your business provides a great opportunity to accomplish things of eternal value! In Revelation 22:12, God said, "Look, I am coming soon! My reward is with me, and I will give to each person according to what they have done."

17. Are You Too Busy to Spend Time With God?

When you're building a business, I understand that you would be extremely busy. However, it is very easy to get so busy that you rarely spend quality time with the Lord in prayer and reading his word. This is common for most Christians, including business people, but it generally results in decisions that are not God's best.

The best business decisions today depend on future events, and so it's important to remember that only God knows the future. A good example is provided in 2 Kings 7:1–20, where Elisha predicted that the price of food would drop significantly, and indeed it did.

So, given that only God knows the future, wise Christian business owners take the time to pray and ask God for his wisdom and specific direction. In Isaiah 48:17, God said, "I am the Lord your God, who teaches you what is best for you, who directs you in the way you should go."

What an awesome promise from the Lord! Let's spend quality time with him in prayer, reading his word, and seeking biblical counsel in order to discern exactly what God wants us to do before making any major business or financial decision!

18. God Gives Us the Ability to Earn Income from Our Businesses

Deuteronomy 8:17–18, provides this warning to those who are successful: "You may say to yourself, 'My power and the strength of my hands have produced this wealth for me.' But remember the Lord your God, for it is he who gives you the ability to produce wealth."

And 1 Corinthians 4:7 states, "For who makes you different from anyone else? What do you have that you did not receive? And if you did receive it, why do you boast as though you did not?" Further, Ephesians 2:10 states, "For we are God's handiwork, created in Christ Jesus to do good works, which God prepared in advance for us to do."

In conclusion, as God's workmanship, we must acknowledge in our hearts and minds that God gave us all of our natural abilities, including the ability to manage a business and earn a very good income. Therefore, we must humbly thank God for his blessings and as stewards, utilize our natural abilities and money in accordance with God's principles and specific will.

Our perspective should imitate the attitude reflected in Psalm 107:8–9: "Let them give thanks to the LORD for his unfailing love and his wonderful deeds for mankind, for he satisfies the thirsty and fills the hungry with good things."

19. Use Minimal Debt in Your Business

With respect to business finances, the world's mindset is that smart people use other people's money. In other words, it's a good idea to use debt aggressively to expand your business. This worldly thinking is contrary to God's word because the Lord discouraged debt and warned how dangerous it is (Proverbs 22:7). Throughout Scripture, God met needs with no debt.

Further, in Deuteronomy 28:1–12, God promised his people:

> If you fully obey the LORD your God and carefully follow all his commands I give you today, the LORD your God will set you high above all the nations on earth. All these blessings will come on you and accompany you if you obey the LORD your God …
>
> The LORD will send a blessing on your barns and on everything you put your hand to …
>
> The LORD will open the heavens, the storehouse of his bounty, to send rain on your land in season and to bless all the work of your hands. You will lend to many nations but will borrow from none.

Later on, in verse 15, God warned that if we don't fully obey him, we will be borrowers and not lenders.

In summary, smart people do not use other people's money; rather, smart people use as little debt as possible and pay it off as quickly as possible.

20. God Meets Business Needs With No Debt

God can meet your business needs with no debt. Here's an example from Luke: "He said to Simon, 'Put out into deep water, and let down the nets for a catch.' Simon answered, 'Master, we've worked hard all night and haven't caught anything'" (Luke 5:4–5).

Let me provide a comment here. Simon Peter could very easily have said something like "No, Jesus, my expertise is in fishing, and yours is in carpentry. I know from decades of experience that it is difficult to impossible to catch fish during the daytime. The best time to catch them is at night, so it does not make sense to put out the nets for a catch in the daytime."

However, Simon Peter didn't do that; rather, he obeyed the Lord. The story goes on to say in Luke 5:5–9:

> "But because you say so, I will let down the nets."
>
> When they had done so, they caught such a large number of fish that their nets began to break. So they signaled their partners in the other boat to come and help them, and they came and filled both boats so full that they began to sink.
>
> When Simon Peter saw this, he fell at Jesus' knees and said, "Go away from me, Lord; I am a sinful man!" For he and all his companions were astonished at the catch of fish they had taken.

In summary, before borrowing any money or making any major business financial decision for your business, pray and ask

God to provide. Generally, God will provide in a way that is glorifying to him.

21. Business Cash Flow Planning

Very few (and I mean very few) business owners have a corporate budget or cash flow plan, and as a result, sometimes they make bad business decisions. Proverbs 21:5 says, "The plans of the diligent lead to profit as surely as haste leads to poverty."

Making an important financial decision, such as expanding your business without preparing a corporate budget or cash flow beforehand, can be disastrous. It is no wonder that God admonishes us to plan ahead.

In Luke 14:28–30, Jesus said:

> Suppose one of you wants to build a tower. Won't you first sit down and estimate the cost to see if you have enough money to complete it? For if you lay the foundation and are not able to finish it, everyone who sees it will ridicule you, saying, "This person began to build and wasn't able to finish."

If you're a business owner and you want to build your business, remember that Christ admonished us to plan ahead. The most practical way to do that is to develop and implement a corporate budget or cash flow plan.

22. God's Perspective Versus the World's Perspective on Business Borrowing

God's perspective with respect to both business and personal finances is for us to save for future needs; meanwhile, the world's perspective is to buy now and pay later.

Here's something to think about. God is in control. "The LORD has established His throne in the heavens, and His sovereignty rules over all" (Psalm 103:19, NASB). And God (not the bank) has promised to meet our business and personal needs if we put him first. In Philippians 4:19, Paul said, "My God will meet all your needs according to the riches of his glory in Christ Jesus."

Is it not reasonable, then, for Christian business people to trust God to meet the company's needs rather than relying on bank loans, credit cards, stretching one's suppliers, or lease financing? "Trust in the LORD with all your heart, and lean not on your own understanding; in all your ways acknowledge Him, and He shall direct your paths" (Proverbs 3:5–6, NKJV).

23. How Mr. Wise and Mr. Unwise Approach Business Finances

Here is a comparison for business owners where "Mr. Wise" takes a biblical approach and "Mr. Unwise" takes a worldly approach.

"Mr. Wise" habitually saves for future business and personal needs. He focuses on needs, not wants and desires. Generally, he buys used vehicles with no debt. He saves a significant down payment for his home and office building and pays down his mortgage as soon as possible. He uses a credit card carefully, pays it off each month, and incurs no interest charges. He also follows a cash flow plan/budget both corporately and personally.

"Mr. Unwise" habitually borrows money and rarely saves for future business or personal needs. He often buys things he does not need. He purchases new vehicles every three to four years, with debt. He also buys a home and office building with small down payments and takes on big mortgages. He uses a credit card freely and generally runs a balance. Further, he has no cash flow plan/budget at either the corporate or personal level.

Are you wise or unwise in managing your business and personal finances?

24. Case Study: Business Debt Restructuring

Joe owns and manages his own business. When he started several years ago, he had no savings, so he increased his personal line of credit and invested the funds into his new company. Within one year, these funds had been used, so he obtained a business line of credit.

Initially, Joe believed he had solved his company's financial problems. However, over the next two years, the business line of credit gradually increased to its limit.

To solve this problem, Joe obtained a second mortgage on his home and used the funds to pay down his business line of credit.

As can be seen, Joe is restructuring his debt, believing that he is solving his corporate financial problems, when in fact, the underlying problem is that there is more money going out than coming in. Joe needs to develop and implement a projected cash flow plan for his company to ensure it has a monthly surplus to pay down debt and save for future needs.

25. Practical Steps to Eliminate Corporate Debt

If you're a business owner, here are some suggestions to reduce your corporate debt.

1. Prayerfully ask God for his wisdom (James 1:5) and specific direction (Psalm 25:12) as to what you should do to become debt-free.
2. Since only God knows the future, depend on him to help you make wise business decisions (Genesis 41).

3. Save during the good times in order to have sufficient funds during the bad times (Proverbs 21:20).

4. Meditate upon God's word with respect to business finances (Hebrews 4:12) and allow the Lord, through his word and Spirit, to change the way you think (Romans 12:2) with respect to the management of business finances.

5. Develop and implement a corporate cash flow plan to ensure your company spends less than its revenue so it has a surplus to pay down debt (Luke 14:28–30).

6. Ask God to enable you to be content with his provision (Luke 3:14).

7. Depending upon God, follow up and persevere until your company is totally debt-free (Isaiah 46:4).

26. Do Not Presume on the Future

Here are some Scripture verses that apply to business finances. James 4:13–15 warns:

> Now listen, you who say, "Today or tomorrow we will go to this or that city, spend a year there, carry on business and make money." Why, you do not even know what will happen tomorrow. What is your life? You are a mist that appears for a little while and then vanishes. Instead, you ought to say, "If it is the Lord's will, we will live and do this or that."

In addition, Ecclesiastes 8:7 states, "Since no one knows the future, who can tell someone else what is to come?" So often, Christian business owners presume on the future and make decisions based upon their own limited resources rather than going to the God of the universe, the King of kings and the Lord of lords, who knows the future (Isaiah 46:10). Our God knows what the best business decisions are from a long-term perspective.

Hence, there is no substitute for investing quality time with the Lord in prayer, asking him for his specific direction (Psalm 32:8), and then diligently implementing his will for the business God has entrusted to you (Joshua 24:24).

27. Minimize Your Corporate and Personal Taxes

Jesus said, "Give back to Caesar what is Caesar's, and to God what is God's" (Matthew 22:21). Christian business owners must pay their corporate and personal taxes. However, the wise steward minimizes these taxes by obtaining professional tax advice. Here are seven tax planning ideas from a Canadian perspective.

1. Determine the best way to take income from your company, such as salary, dividends, or drawdown of share-holders loan account.
2. Trigger capital gains in your corporation and pay tax-free dividends via the capital dividend account.
3. Generally, pay donations personally.
4. Crystallize your capital gains exemption.
5. Use a family trust to income split.
6. Accumulate retirement savings at the low business rate in your operating company and take dividends when your income is lower in retirement.
7. Acquire depreciable assets prior to your fiscal year-end.

If you would like Canadian tax planning advice for your business, feel free to send me an email at tcopland@zing-net.ca.

28. Avoid Personal Guarantees

Most banks ask the business owner to provide a personal guarantee for corporate debt. God instructs otherwise. "It's a dangerous thing to guarantee payment for someone's debts. Don't do it!" (Proverbs 11:15, CEV). Another passage later in Proverbs warns, "Don't guarantee to pay someone else's debt. If you don't have the money, you might lose your bed" (Proverbs 22:26–27, CEV).

In other words, you could lose something important to you, such as your home or your retirement fund, if you provide your personal guarantee for corporate debt. Here are some ideas to free yourself (Proverbs 6:1–5) from corporate guarantees:

1. Lower the company's debt-to-equity ratio by investing personal cash into the company, following a personal budget, reducing your salary, or selling unnecessary assets and paying down debt.
2. Switch to another bank that is willing to provide the loan with no personal guarantees.
3. Obtain equity investors.

And if you absolutely must personally guarantee some corporate debt, have one spouse as the guarantor and the other spouse own the family home to avoid the risk of losing your home. The intent is not to avoid having to pay your debts but rather to protect your home, which is the most important asset to the family.

Since I began my practice in 1977, I've seen too many families get evicted from their homes because the family business encountered financial problems, and the parents had provided personal guarantees or specific collateral charges on the family home. For sure, do everything you can to protect your family's home.

29. Focus on Your Area of Expertise

I've seen many cases where entrepreneurs get involved in a business where they have limited knowledge, generally resulting in losses. "It is dangerous to have zeal without knowledge, and the one who acts hastily makes poor choices" (Proverbs 19:2, NET). In other words, it's not good to have excitement and get involved in a particular business if you do not thoroughly understand it.

Given that many business people were farmers at the time when the proverbs were written, God admonished us to stick with the businesses that we know and understand. Proverbs 28:19–20 says, "Those who work their land will have abundant food, but those who chase fantasies will have their fill of poverty. A faithful person will be richly blessed, but one eager to get rich will not go unpunished."

In summary, focus on the business God has called you to be involved in, and do not get sidetracked into businesses where you have limited experience or knowledge.

30. Summary: God's Financial Wisdom for Business

Here's a summary of the biblical financial principles that apply to business.

1. Acknowledge that you are a steward of God's business (Haggai 2:8) and therefore manage his business in accordance with the Lord's financial principles (Luke 22:42).
2. Prayerfully develop a close relationship with the Lord so you can discern his specific will (Psalm 32:8) before making any major business decision.
3. Use minimal corporate debt and pay down your corporate and personal debt as soon as possible (Proverbs 22:7).

4. Avoid giving personal guarantees for corporate debt (Proverbs 11:15).
5. Use your business for ministry as the Lord directs, such as giving to God's work (Proverbs 3:9–10), using the office facilities for discipleship, and witnessing to employees, clients, and suppliers.
6. Minimize your corporate and personal taxes by obtaining professional tax advice (Matthew 22:21).
7. Prepare and implement a corporate cash flow plan to ensure you spend less than you earn and have a surplus to pay down debt and save for future needs (Proverbs 21:20).

To learn more about what the Bible says on business finances, be sure to watch the seven half-hour video series titled "God's Financial Wisdom for Business" and check out our other resources at www.coplandfinancialministries.org. If you have a specific question, send me an email at tcopland@zing-net.ca. You can also follow @biblefinance on Facebook, Instagram, and Twitter.

XIX.
DEVELOPING A GODLY ATTITUDE TOWARD MONEY

1. Money Is Neutral

Money is neither moral nor immoral. Money is neither spiritual nor unspiritual. It can be used to further God's kingdom, or it can be used for evil. In fact, money is neutral. There is nothing inherently good or bad about money in and of itself.

However, God is concerned about our attitudes or motives toward money. For example, in 1 Timothy 6:9–10, Paul warned of the dangers of the love of money.

> Those who want to get rich fall into temptation and a trap and into many foolish and harmful desires that plunge people into ruin and destruction. For the love of money is a root of all kinds of evil. Some people, eager for money, have wandered from the faith and pierced themselves with many griefs.

It is not money itself but "the love of money" that is the root of all kinds of evil. The love of money is reflected in an individual through covetousness, selfishness, greed, pride, and lack of contentment. If you consistently struggle with these worldly attitudes, they will destroy your finances and often your relationship with your spouse.

I encourage you to prayerfully read relevant Scriptures that apply to money and ask God if you have an issue with the love of money, perhaps represented by one of the worldly attitudes outlined above.

2. The Love of Money

In 1 Timothy 6:9–10, Paul warned that even Christians can struggle with the love of money.

Some indicators of the love of money include excessive hard work (Proverbs 23:4–5), little involvement in ministry (Ephesians 2:10), limited time with God (John 10:27), giving little to God's work (Proverbs 3:9–10), and a selfish lifestyle (Luke 12:15–21).

Regardless of how much money and material things you accumulate, in Ecclesiastes 5:10, God warned that the love of money will never be satisfied. "Whoever loves money never has money enough; whoever loves wealth is never satisfied with their income."

What's the solution? Jesus told us to get our priorities right when he said, "Love the Lord your God with all your heart and with all your soul and with all your mind" (Matthew 22:37).

In other words, focus on God's priorities (things that have eternal significance like the salvation of people and contributing to God's work) not temporal things such as money and material things.

3. It Isn't Wrong to Have a Lot of Money

It is not wrong for a Christian to have a lot of money. Abraham, David, and Job are examples of godly men to whom God entrusted significant wealth. Because of their godly attitudes, they obediently used money in accordance with God's principles and God's will.

There are successful Christian entrepreneurs today who have godly attitudes and motives toward money. In their hearts and minds, they acknowledge God's ownership of their business; as a result, they live significantly below their means and give generously to God's work. In some cases, these individuals give as much as 75 per cent of their income.

Some Christians with modest incomes have godly attitudes toward money. They are content with God's provision and focus on things of eternal value, such as evangelism and discipleship, rather than material things. Colossians 3:2 says, "Set your minds on things above, not on earthly things."

I encourage you—do not focus on how much money you have. Rather, ask God to help you assess your attitude toward money. This will determine how you use the money that God entrusts to you.

4. Worldly Attitudes Versus Godly Attitudes

A Christian can have worldly attitudes or godly attitudes toward money and material things. For example, selfishness, covetousness, greed, pride, and lack of contentment are all worldly attitudes. If any of these attitudes dominate your thinking, the consequences will be detrimental.

The corresponding godly attitudes with respect to money include selflessness, thankfulness to God, generosity, humility, and contentment. As indicated in Romans 8:6, godly thinking will enable you to experience God's peace in the area of finances. Proverbs 16:2 makes it clear that our attitudes or motives are very important to God. "All a person's ways seem pure to them, but motives are weighed by the LORD."

I encourage you to prayerfully ask God to reveal your motives toward money. King David said, "Search me, God, and know my heart; test me and know my anxious thoughts. See if there is any offensive way in me, and lead me in the way everlasting" (Psalm 139:23–24).

5. Struggling With Worldly Attitudes

When a Christian struggles with covetousness, selfishness, greed, or other worldly attitudes toward money, Paul explained that the underlying cause is a spiritual struggle between God's Holy Spirit and our sinful nature.

> So I say, walk by the Spirit, and you will not gratify the desires of the flesh. For the flesh desires what is contrary to the Spirit, and the Spirit what is contrary to the flesh. They are in conflict with each other, so that you are not to do whatever you want. But if you are led by the Spirit, you are not under the law. (Galatians 5:16–18)

You can win this spiritual struggle by depending on God's Holy Spirit to guide you. This requires a close personal relationship with the Lord Jesus Christ. In John 15:5, Jesus said, "I am the vine; you are the branches. If you remain in me and I in you, you will bear much fruit; apart from me you can do nothing."

In summary, you can overcome worldly attitudes or motives by developing and maintaining a close personal relationship with Jesus Christ.

6. Contentment Is the Antidote to Many Worldly Attitudes

Common worldly attitudes toward money and material things include covetousness, selfishness, greed, and lack of contentment. Fortunately, learning contentment will enable a Christian to defeat these worldly attitudes.

Even Paul found that it is necessary to learn to be content. In Philippians 4:11–13, he said:

> I have learned to be content whatever the circumstances. I know what it is to be in need, and I know what it is to have plenty. I have learned the secret of being content in any

and every situation, whether well fed or hungry, whether living in plenty or in want. I can do all this through him who gives me strength.

What was Paul's "secret" to learning contentment? It was his close personal relationship with Jesus Christ. Why? Because as we focus on our relationship with Christ and gain an eternal perspective, temporal things such as money become much less important to us.

Colossians 3:2 says, "Set your minds on things above, not on earthly things." I encourage you to prayerfully ask God to enable you to learn to be content with his provision. One thing that can help is to remember that God promises to meet your needs (Matthew 6:31–33) but not necessarily your wants and desires. So focus on spending money only on your needs.

7. Dealing With Worldly Attitudes

Having counselled thousands of people since 1982, I found that the underlying cause for financial problems was a worldly mindset toward money and material things. For example, some struggle with selfishness or covetousness and, as a result, spend more than they earn and accumulate debt. Others are like the rich fool in Luke 12 and have trusted in money and material things; when they lose these things, they are devastated.

What's the solution for dealing with a worldly mindset? Romans 12:2 admonishes us, "Do not conform to the pattern of this world, but be transformed by the renewing of your mind."

How do we renew our minds? Joshua 1:8 states, "Keep this Book of the Law always on your lips; meditate on it day and night, so that you may be careful to do everything written in it. Then you will be prosperous and successful."

In summary, meditating on God's word will enable Christians to develop godly mindsets and attitudes toward money.

8. Case Study: Rick and Judy Struggle With Covetousness

Rick and Judy consistently notice the nicer things that others have. One of their many desires is to own a larger home, even though their present home meets their needs. Rick almost always wants a more expensive car, and Judy has accumulated more clothes than she'll ever need. Notwithstanding their above-average incomes, because of their desires, they have accumulated significant debt.

The biblical truth is that Rick and Judy are both struggling with covetousness and a lack of contentment. In Exodus 20:17, God said, "You shall not covet your neighbor's house. You shall not covet your neighbor's wife, or his male or female servant, his ox or donkey, or anything that belongs to your neighbor."

As Paul indicated in Philippians 4:11–13, Rick and Judy need to learn to be content and to live within the income that God has provided. How do you learn to be content? The key is to develop a close personal relationship with Jesus Christ (Philippians 4:13) and focus on things of eternal value, not things that are temporal (Colossians 3:1–2).

9. Case Study: Steve Believes Money Will Bring Happiness

Each year, Steve works harder and longer hours, believing that the accumulation of money and material things will bring happiness and peace of mind. Even though he has been a Christian for over ten years, Steve rarely has a quiet time with the Lord and has limited involvement in ministry.

Steve is like the seed that fell among thorns in Matthew 13:22. "The seed falling among the thorns refers to someone who hears the word, but the worries of this life and the deceitfulness of wealth choke the word, making it unfruitful."

Without realizing it, Steve believes the lie that money will provide happiness and peace. As a result, he has not grown spiritually, and he is not doing anything significant for the Lord's work.

God's truth is that happiness and peace can be received only through a close personal relationship with Jesus Christ. In John 14:27, Jesus said, "Peace I leave with you; my peace I give you. I do not give to you as the world gives. Do not let your hearts be troubled and do not be afraid."

In conclusion, we must purposely develop our relationships with Jesus Christ.

10. Case Study: Jane Demonstrates Godly Attitudes Toward Money

Jane is a single woman who earns an average income. She spends wisely, stays within her budget, and tithes faithfully. Although she lives modestly, she's content with God's provision. Jane is not concerned that most of her friends have more material things. Rather, the focus of her time and energy is ministering to others through her local church.

Whenever Jane has a financial need that is beyond her means, she doesn't look for other sources of income or borrow the money. Instead, she prayerfully asks God to provide and then waits for his provision. Her faith in God has been strengthened on many occasions when the Lord has provided in an unusual way.

Jane's story exemplifies the following godly attitudes toward money. She is content (1 Timothy 6:6–8) and thankful for God's provision (Psalm 107:8–9). She puts God first and trusts God to meet her needs (Matthew 6:31–33). Jane tithes faithfully (Proverbs 3:9–10) and lives within a budget (Luke 14:28–30).

And perhaps most importantly, Jane is focused on things of eternal value (Colossians 3:1–2), such as ministering to others.

11. Case Study: John and Mary Put God First in Operating Their Business

When John and Mary started their business, the profits were low and cash flow was tight. Nevertheless, they honoured God by giving him 10 per cent of their profits. They acknowledged God's ownership of their business and prayed daily for his wisdom. Among other things, God directed them to limit their personal lifestyle, even if their income increased.

Over the next several years, God blessed their business beyond their imagination. As a result, John and Mary currently give 70 per cent of their income to God's work. They praise God for enabling them to do this. They continue to live in their middle-class home and drive used cars. Their friends and relatives have no idea that God has blessed their business and enabled them to give so generously.

John and Mary's story exemplifies the following godly attitudes toward money. They were humble (James 4:10) because they did not reveal their substantial profits or generous giving to others (Matthew 6:1–4). They acknowledged God's ownership of their business (Psalm 24:1–2). They were content to limit their lifestyle and give generously to God's work (2 Corinthians 9:6–11).

I encourage you to develop and maintain some of the godly attitudes that John and Mary have demonstrated, and God will bless you both here on earth and in eternity (Matthew 16:27).

12. The Mind Controlled by the Spirit

In Romans 8:5, God made it clear that how we think will determine what we do in many areas, including managing money. Here's what Scripture says: "Those who live according to the flesh have their minds set on what the flesh desires; but those who live in accordance with the Spirit have their minds set on what the Spirit desires."

For example, if we allow our minds to think in a worldly fashion, then we will manage money in the same way. Consider the following questions:

1. Are you more influenced by the mainstream culture or God's word when it comes to managing money?
2. Do you struggle with covetousness, selfishness, or greed? Or are you content with God's provision?
3. Do you desire to have more material things, or to give more to God's work?
4. Do you regularly fill your mind with what the Bible says about finances?
5. In Romans 8:6, God promised that "the mind controlled by the Spirit is life and peace." Are you experiencing God's peace in the area of finances?

In summary, allow your mind to be controlled by the Holy Spirit, and read God's word often, particularly with respect to finances. Then you will manage money God's way and experience the Lord's peace in the area of finances.

In order to learn more about God's word on finances and to help you develop a godly mindset with respect to money and material things, check out our numerous resources available at www.coplandfinancialministries.org. Follow @biblefinance on Facebook, Instagram, and Twitter.

XX.
MONEY MANAGEMENT IMPACTS ETERNITY

1. Build Up Treasures in Heaven

Jesus said in Matthew 6:19–21:

> "Do not store up for yourselves treasures on earth, where moths and vermin destroy, and where thieves break in and steal. But store up for yourselves treasures in heaven, where moths and vermin do not destroy, and where thieves do not break in and steal. For where your treasure is, there your heart will be also."

Treasures in heaven represent those things we will treasure when we get to heaven, such as the salvation of people, our personal relationship with Jesus Christ, God's peace (John 14:27), God's joy (Psalm 16:11), and the rewards that he promises to his faithful servants (Matthew 25:21).

On the other hand, treasures on earth represent those things we tend to value while we are here on earth, including money and temporary pleasures; however, they are very temporary in nature, as we will lose them after we die.

As Christians, we need to focus on building up treasures in heaven rather than treasures on earth.

2. Your Heart Follows What You Treasure

In Matthew 6, Jesus admonished us to build up treasures in heaven rather than treasures on earth. In other words, focus on things of eternal value, such as the salvation of people, involvement in ministry, and giving to God's work, rather than focusing on accumulating money and material things. The latter are temporary in nature.

Further, Jesus warned, "For where your treasure is, there your heart will be also" (Matthew 6:21). In other words, Christ is saying what you really treasure is generally reflected in where you spend your money and your time. Regardless of what we may say, our bank accounts, credit cards, and day-timers reflect our true priorities.

If, like most people, you've been building up treasures on earth rather than treasures in heaven, I suggest that you pray, meditate upon God's word with respect to finances, and start investing your money and time in God's work, because often your heart will follow where you invest your money and your time (Matthew 6:21).

3. Avoid the Love of Money

In 1 Timothy 6:9–10, Paul warned:

> Those who want to get rich fall into temptation and a trap and into many foolish and harmful desires that plunge people into ruin and destruction. For the love of money is a root of all kinds of evil. Some people, eager for money, have wandered from the faith and pierced themselves with many griefs.

Note that even Christians can have a problem with this; and it is the *love* of money that is a root of all kinds of evil, not money in and of itself. Worldly attitudes such as covetousness, selfishness, greed, pride, and envy will often reflect the love of money in an individual.

In the next verse, Paul instructed Timothy, "But you, man of God, flee from all this, and pursue righteousness, godliness, faith, love, endurance and gentleness" (1 Timothy 6:11). The pursuit of godly characteristics such as righteousness, godliness, faith, love, endurance, and gentleness will result in rewards in heaven and help you avoid the love of money.

4. Be Sure to Serve God and Not Money

In Matthew 6:24, Jesus said, "No one can serve two masters. Either you will hate the one and love the other, or you will be devoted to the one and despise the other. You cannot serve both God and money."

Money and material things can easily become our master and a distraction from many things of eternal value—such as your relationship with Christ, your spouse, your children, ministry work, or investing money in God's ministries.

Here are five indicators that you could be serving money rather than God.

1. You work excessively hard (Proverbs 23:4–5).
2. You have very limited or no time with God each day (John 10:27).
3. You have little or no involvement in ministry (Ephesians 2:10).
4. You give very little to God's work (Proverbs 3:9–10).
5. You have a selfish lifestyle with no desire to give to God's work (see the parable of the rich fool in Luke 12:15–21).

In summary, prayerfully ask God to enable you to focus on serving him rather than money and material things.

5. Your Relationship With Christ Should Be Your Highest Priority

In the parable of the hidden treasure, Jesus said: "The kingdom of heaven is like treasure hidden in a field. When a man found it, he hid it again, and then in his joy went and sold all he had and bought that field" (Matthew 13:44).

God is saying that the kingdom of heaven is of such great value that, if need be, we should be willing to give up everything we have on this earth in order to have the kingdom of heaven. This heavenly kingdom includes the greatest treasure of all—a personal relationship with Jesus Christ, not only here on earth but also for eternity in heaven!

Paul considered his relationship with Christ to be more important than anything else. In Philippians 3:8, Paul said, "What is more, I consider everything a loss because of the surpassing worth of knowing Christ Jesus my Lord, for whose sake I have lost all things. I consider them garbage, that I may gain Christ."

In summary, make your relationship with Christ your highest priority!

6. The Best Investment: It's Guaranteed by God!

Jesus said in Matthew 19:29, "Everyone who has left houses … or fields for my sake will receive a hundred times as much and will inherit eternal life."

What a promise from God! We can give up money and material things (such as houses and fields, which are temporary in nature) and receive a hundred times as much in eternity, and it's guaranteed by God!

Please understand, I'm not teaching the prosperity gospel. It is not appropriate for you to give money to God's work and then demand that he give you in return a hundred times as much. God will not be manipulated by us. But rather, he wants us to give to his work out of our love for him and expect nothing in return, as Jesus talked about in Luke 6.

However, if a Christian does manage money according to biblical principles, including giving generously to God's work (with the right heart), then, as indicated in the parable of the ten minas (Luke 19:11–27), God may very well entrust you with even more.

7. Parable of the Talents

In Matthew 25, Jesus told a story of a master (who is God) who entrusted five talents to one servant, two to another, and one to a third servant. In this story, the servants are you and I. Scripture that says after a long time (perhaps a lifetime?) God returned and made the servants accountable, not for 10 per cent of what they had but rather for 100 per cent of what God had entrusted to them.

To two servants, God said, "Well done, good and faithful servant! You have been faithful with a few things; I will put you in charge of many things. Come and share your master's happiness!" (Matthew 25:21). As for the third servant who was wicked and lazy, God took away his talent and gave it to the first servant, who was faithful to the Lord.

Therefore, at some point in the future, all of us will be accountable to God for everything he entrusted to us. We do not know when that day of accountability is coming—it could be when Jesus Christ returns or after we die and stand before the Lord at the judgment seat of Christ (2 Corinthians 5:10).

Either way, the most important thing for us as Christians is to ensure we are utilizing the money and material things that God has entrusted to us according to his principles and his specific will.

8. There Will Be Rewards in Heaven for Biblical Money Management and Godly Character

In Matthew 16:27, Jesus said, "The Son of Man is going to come in his Father's glory with his angels, and then he will reward each person according to what they have done." It is important to note that many of those rewards in heaven will come as a result of managing money according to biblical principles and God's specific will.

God will also provide rewards in heaven for godly character. 2 Peter 1:5–11 states:

> For this very reason, make every effort to add to your faith goodness; and to goodness, knowledge; and to knowledge, self-control; and to self-control, perseverance; and to perseverance, godliness; and to godliness, mutual affection; and to mutual affection, love. For if you possess these qualities in increasing measure, they will keep you from being ineffective and unproductive in your knowledge of our Lord Jesus Christ …
>
> For if you do these things, you will never stumble, and you will receive a rich welcome into the eternal kingdom of our Lord and Savior Jesus Christ.

What could be better than that!

In conclusion, I encourage you to meditate upon Scripture, especially the godly characteristics that are mentioned. And, depending upon God, ask the Lord to enable you to display those godly characteristics.

9. Remember: Money and Material Things Are Temporary

In 1 Timothy 6:6–8, Paul said, "Godliness with contentment is great gain. For we brought nothing into the world, and we can take nothing out of it. But if we have food and clothing, we will be content with that."

Ecclesiastes 5:15 says, "Everyone comes naked from their mother's womb, and as everyone comes, so they depart. They take nothing from their toil that they can carry in their hands." It's so important to understand that whatever you have on this earth, you will lose when you die. But whatever you give in Christ's name with a godly motive will ultimately come back to you in heaven a hundredfold (Matthew 19:29).

Yes, it's true you cannot take it with you, but by managing money God's way and giving generously to God's work, in a sense, you can "send it on ahead." How? By investing the money that God has entrusted to you in such a way that it will result in eternal benefits for you and the people who are blessed by your giving.

10. Be Sure to Keep Eternity in Mind

Many Christians save for retirement, which is consistent with biblical principles (Luke 14:28–30). The advice often given by financial advisers is to invest with a 30-year time horizon. This is fine with respect to saving for retirement, but as Christians, we should be investing with a time horizon of eternity.

So ask yourself this question—what are you doing today with the money God has entrusted to you that will have an eternal impact? In Philippians 4:17, Paul said that as you give to God's work, it is credited to your heavenly account.

In other words, God is keeping track of what we do for him and how we invest and use his money (Haggai 2:8). Think of it, each time you give to God's work, there is a credit to your heavenly account that you and many others will benefit from when you get to heaven!

In summary, investing in God's work is an excellent way to convert a temporal asset such as money into something of eternal value!

11. Make the Paradigm Shift

In my experience, very few Christians can be entrusted with a lot of money. This is because when most people receive more money, they raise their standard of living rather than raising their standard of giving. Raising one's standard of living or even hoarding money and material things will result in *no rewards* in heaven.

Once Christians understand they are stewards of God's money and that there will be incredible rewards in heaven for using money for eternal purposes, they need to study and apply what God's word says about finances. They should also prayerfully discern God's specific will in using the money he has entrusted to them.

Unfortunately, today most Christians manage and use money much the way non-believers do, often buying things they don't need on credit and accumulating debt. As the debt goes up, their giving inevitably goes down.

In summary, all Christians need to make the paradigm shift from focusing on temporal things to focusing on using money in ways that will have an impact for eternity.

12. Heaven Is Our Home, Not Earth

We tend to store up treasures here on earth because most people think of Earth as being their home. The truth is that Earth is not our home; we are on this earth for a relatively short period of time compared to eternity in heaven.

As described in Hebrews 11:13–16, the patriarchs lived as "foreigners and strangers on earth." The passage goes on to say, "Instead, they were longing for a better country—a heavenly one."

In other words, these great men of God recognized that Earth was not their home, just a temporary place where they would sojourn while they were alive. But more importantly, their eternal destiny and eternal home were in heaven.

In Philippians 3:20, Paul said, "Our citizenship is in heaven. And we eagerly await a Savior from there, the Lord Jesus Christ." As Christians, we need to remember that our home and citizenship are in heaven, not on this earth. So it only makes sense to invest money and time into ministries that will result in rewards in heaven, which will be of eternal benefit!

13. Moderate Your Lifestyle Like Moses

Moses was a godly man who had his priorities right with respect to money and material things. "He chose to be mistreated along with the people of God rather than to enjoy the fleeting pleasures of sin. He regarded disgrace for the sake of Christ as of greater value than the treasures of Egypt, because he was looking ahead to his reward" (Hebrews 11:25–26).

In other words, Moses understood that heaven, not Earth, was his home. Therefore, he knew he should use the time, money, and resources that God entrusted to him in order to serve the Lord faithfully, because "he was looking ahead to his reward" in heaven.

In order for any Christian to receive rewards in heaven, faithfulness to God is essential. As 1 Corinthians 4:2 states, "Now it is required that those who have been given a trust must prove faithful."

Here is an extremely important question: Are you using the money, time, and talents that God has entrusted to you for eternal purposes or for selfish purposes?

14. How You Manage Money Impacts Eternity

Here's a key question: Does how you manage money impact eternity? The answer is, absolutely yes.

For example, let's suppose you acknowledge you are a steward of God's resources (Haggai 2:8) and learn and apply biblical financial principles. These principles include following a budget (Luke 14:28–30) and being content with God's provision (1 Timothy 6:6–8). They also include having minimal debt and being able to give generously to God's work as a result (2 Corinthians 9:6–11).

We know that God's word is powerful (Hebrews 4:12); therefore, some people will be led to accept Christ as Saviour and Lord and be discipled. Evangelizing and discipling people has an eternal impact because there will be people in heaven (who otherwise may not be there) thanking you for the money you gave and the time and effort you put forth that contributed to their salvation. The salvation of an individual lasts for eternity and the rewards that you will receive in heaven for your godly management of money will also last for eternity (Matthew 16:27).

In summary, remind yourself daily that how you utilize the money and material things God has entrusted to you can have an eternal impact if you invest that money God's way.

15. Our Lives on Earth Compared to Eternity

Most people live to reach the age of sixty to one hundred. So clearly, our lives here on earth are extremely short compared to the time we will spend in heaven. How long will we be in heaven?

Perhaps ten million years? Maybe ten billion years? No, it's longer—it is for eternity! It never ends!

That's why James describes us as "a mist that appears for a little while and then vanishes" (James 4:14). Consider the reality of what Moses said, "Teach us to number our days, so that we may gain a heart of wisdom" (Psalm 90:12).

Our time here on earth is extremely short compared to eternity in heaven; however, how we use the resources God has entrusted to us (including our money, time, and talents) will have a huge impact for eternity. If we are good stewards of everything God has entrusted to us, including giving to his work, there will be huge rewards in heaven that we can enjoy forever!

16. Warning: God Will Judge Everyone

The Bible teaches about two eternal judgments—one for the believer and one for the non-believer. All true believers will pass the judgment of faith in Christ at the great white throne, and all non-believers will fail the judgment of faith in Christ because their names were not written in the book of life (Revelation 20:11–15).

For clarity, Jesus said, "Do not be amazed at this, for a time is coming when all who are in their graves will hear his voice and come out—those who have done what is good will rise to live, and those who have done what is evil will rise to be condemned" (John 5:28–29).

However, when Christians get to heaven, faith is not the only thing that will be judged. Christians will also be judged for their works. At the judgment seat of Christ (2 Corinthians 5:10), Christians will be given rewards or will suffer loss (1 Corinthians 3:12–15) by way of having fewer rewards in heaven. Further, Christians will be held responsible (Luke 19:11–26) for how we used the money, time, and talents that God entrusted to us.

If you have accepted Jesus Christ as your Saviour and Lord, you will be forgiven for your sin and spend eternity in heaven. However, I encourage you to understand that you will be judged by Jesus Christ and be given rewards or suffer loss based on your faithfulness to God in utilizing the resources the Lord entrusted to you while you are here on earth.

17. God Will Judge Fairly

Although everyone who has accepted Christ as Saviour and Lord will spend eternity in heaven, Scripture indicates that God will judge everyone, including believers (Acts 17:31) and that he will judge fairly (Genesis 18:25). Jeremiah 17:10 states, "I the LORD search the heart and examine the mind, to reward each person according to their conduct, according to what their deeds deserve." God will examine our motives and provide rewards to his children according to how they managed the money, time and talents that God entrusted to them.

And 1 Corinthians 4:5 states, "Therefore judge nothing before the appointed time; wait until the Lord comes. He will bring to light what is hidden in darkness and will expose the motives of the heart. At that time each will receive their praise from God."

Many Christians forget that the rewards or lack of rewards we will receive when we get to heaven will benefit us (and others there) for eternity! Therefore, it makes sense to invest your money, time, and talents into God's work so you will receive many rewards when you get to heaven!

18. We Are All Individually Accountable

Paul said in Romans 14:12, "Each of us will give an account of ourselves to God." And 1 Peter 4:5 states, "They will have to give account to him who is ready to judge the living and the dead."

The living represents those who are spiritually alive, having accepted Christ as their Saviour and Lord. The spiritually dead are those who have never accepted Christ as Saviour and Lord. God will judge both but in very different ways.

Christians will appear before the judgment seat of Christ to receive rewards or suffer the loss of a lack of rewards for their service to God (2 Corinthians 5:10). They will not be condemned (Romans 8:1) but forgiven for their sins and spend eternity in heaven.

As for the non-believers, who are spiritually dead, they will be judged and receive punishment based upon what they did while on earth. God's judgment will be thorough. Ecclesiastes 12:13–14 says, "Fear God and keep his commandments, for this is the duty of all mankind. For God will bring every deed into judgment, including every hidden thing, whether it is good or evil."

In summary, remember that every single one of us on earth is ultimately accountable to the King of kings and the Lord of lords—Jesus Christ himself—for how we use the money, time, and talents that God entrusted to us while we are here on earth.

19. Jesus Will Prepare a Place for Us in Heaven

Many Christians focus on renovating their home or purchasing just the right house. There's nothing wrong with having a nice home, but our homes here on earth are very temporary. The wise Christian invests in God's kingdom, in order to have a great home in heaven for eternity.

Jesus said, "In My Father's house are many mansions; if it were not so, I would have told you. I go to prepare a place for you" (John 14:2, NKJV). For Christians, heaven is our home. Paul said, "As long as we are at home in the body we are away from the Lord. For we live by faith, not by sight. We are confident,

I say, and would prefer to be away from the body and at home with the Lord" (2 Corinthians 5:6–8).

Given that we are going to spend eternity in our heavenly home, it makes sense to invest money in God's work that will have an eternal impact (such as people coming to know Christ). This will result in eternal rewards and very likely a nice home in heaven.

20. The Reward of Rulership

Although Christians will reign with Christ during the millennium (Revelation 20:6), Christ indicated that some will be put "in charge of many things" (Matthew 25:21–23). Some believers will rule over cities. As Luke 19:17–24 describes, one person will rule over ten cities, another will rule over five, while a third won't be entrusted any cities. They will receive responsibility in proportion to their faithfulness in managing money.

All believers will be with Christ in heaven, but there will be different levels of rewards and responsibilities. Revelation 2:26 states, "To the one who is victorious and does my will to the end, I will give authority over the nations." Further, some believers will receive crowns in heaven, which require biblical money management. For example:

1. The crown of rejoicing is given for investing one's time and money into evangelism and discipleship (1 Thessalonians 2:19–20; Philippians 4:1).
2. The crown of glory is given for faithfully serving Christ in a position of spiritual leadership (1 Peter 5:1–4; 1 Timothy 3:3–5).

In summary, Christians need to use God's money his way in order to be eligible for some of the crowns in heaven.

21. Eternal Differences in Heaven

Christians will have different levels of rewards in heaven depending upon their level of faithfulness to God while on this earth. Not every Christian will hear, "Well done, good and faithful servant" (Matthew 25:23). Not all believers will have treasures in heaven (Matthew 6:19–21). Nor will all Christians will have the same position of authority in heaven (Luke 19:17–26).

In Matthew 16:27, Jesus said, "The Son of Man is going to come in his Father's glory with his angels, and then he will reward each person according to what they have done." Although all true believers will spend eternity in heaven; their rewards will be based upon their stewardship of the money, time, and talents God provided to them.

Most Christians do not understand this biblical truth: how you use money and material things while you are here on earth will impact you for eternity in heaven by way of receiving rewards or suffering loss due to lack of rewards from God.

22. Give With Godly Motives

We must give and serve the Lord with godly motives. Proverbs 16:2 says, "All a person's ways seem pure to them, but motives are weighed by the Lord." Giving with a godly motive includes giving out of our love for the Lord and as a way to say thank you for what Jesus did on the cross.

As 1 Corinthians 4:5 states, "Therefore judge nothing before the appointed time; wait until the Lord comes. He will bring to light what is hidden in darkness and will expose the motives of the heart. At that time each will receive their praise from God."

In other words, as we give, we need to ask God to reveal to us if we have any wrong motives for giving. If there are any, then we should pray David's prayer in Psalm 139:23–24, which says,

"Search me, O God, and know my heart; test me and know my anxious thoughts. See if there is any offensive way in me, and lead me in the way everlasting."

23. Management of Money and Its Impact on Eternity
Each of us is individually accountable to God (Romans 14:12). How we manage God's money will impact eternity, resulting in rewards or lack of rewards when we get to heaven (2 Corinthians 5:10). As stewards of God's money (Haggai 2:8), we need to use money and material things according to God's principles and specific will (Psalm 32:8).

We will reap in eternity what we sow here on earth (Galatians 6:7–9). It's true that you can't take it with you, but you can send it on ahead. The missionary and martyr Jim Elliot said, "He is no fool who gives up what he cannot keep to gain what he cannot lose."

Giving to God's work allows you to convert the temporal asset of money into eternal benefits. Therefore, the wise Christian uses the money, time, and talents God entrusted to them for eternal purposes.

24. The Judgment Seat of Christ
"We must all appear before the judgment seat of Christ, so that each of us may receive what is due us for the things done while in the body, whether good or bad" (2 Corinthians 5:10).

It's important to understand that all Christians will stand before Jesus Christ at the judgment seat of Christ. We will receive rewards, or suffer loss due to lack of rewards, for the things we did while we were here on earth, whether good or bad. People who have accepted Jesus Christ as Saviour and Lord will be forgiven for their sins. Christ paid the penalty for us on the cross, and so all Christians will spend eternity in heaven.

However, the rewards distributed by God in heaven at the judgment seat of Christ will be very different for each individual. Those Christians who worked diligently and used the money, time, and talents God entrusted to them for his glory and for eternal purposes will receive great rewards in heaven for eternity!

25. Eternal Consequences of Bad Stewardship

At the judgment seat of Christ (2 Corinthians 5:10), Christians will be judged based on how we used the resources that God entrusted to us.

In 1 Corinthians 3:11–15, Paul said:

For no one can lay any foundation other than the one already laid, which is Jesus Christ. If anyone builds on this foundation using gold, silver, costly stones, wood, hay or straw, their work will be shown for what it is, because the Day will bring it to light. It will be revealed with fire, and the fire will test the quality of each person's work. If what has been built survives, the builder will receive a reward. If it is burned up, the builder will suffer loss but yet will be saved—even though only as one escaping through the flames.

Works are what we did with the money, time, and talents that God entrusted to us. God's fire will reveal their eternal significance. Works represented by gold, silver, and costly stones will benefit us for eternity, but works represented by wood, hay, or straw will be burned up and not rewarded by God.

Therefore, the wise Christian determines what works will result in eternal rewards in heaven and focuses on those works;

obviously, part of this would involve giving your time, talent, and money to God's work.

26. Eternal Rewards for Biblical Money Management
Here are some works that God will reward in heaven.

1. Giving generously to his work leads to rewards. Jesus promised that a believer would receive a hundred times as much for giving money and material things to his work. Giving privately (Matthew 6:1–4) and cheerfully (2 Corinthians 9:6–7) will certainly be rewarded in heaven (Matthew 19:29).

2. God values doing good works. Ephesians 6:8 states, "The Lord will reward each one for whatever good they do."

3. Those who have served faithfully wherever God has called them to minister will receive rewards (Revelation 11:18). This service could be through a church, a parachurch organization, or informally to family, friends, and others (Ephesians 2:10).

4. Giving to the poor is another example. Matthew 19:21 says, "Go, sell your possessions and give to the poor, and you will have treasure in heaven."

5. Jesus promised rewards for helping those who can never repay you. "Although they cannot repay you, you will be repaid at the resurrection of the righteous" (Luke 14:14).

6. Rewards are also promised for those who endure difficult circumstances (Hebrews 10:34–36).

7. Works resulting in the salvation of people, including giving money and time to evangelical organizations

and witnessing for Christ. A person's salvation will last for eternity.

8. Finally, a life of godliness will be richly rewarded (2 Peter 3:11–14.)
9. Actions done for the Lord with a godly motive will be rewarded (Proverbs 16:2).

Therefore, the wise Christian follows Paul's instructions. "Let us throw off everything that hinders and the sin that so easily entangles. And let us run with perseverance the race marked out for us, fixing our eyes on Jesus, the pioneer and perfecter of faith" (Hebrews 12:1–2).

In summary, use the money, time, and talents God has entrusted to you for his glory, and God will bless you with rewards in heaven for eternity!

27. Determine God's Calling and Fulfill It

Besides using money according to God's specific will, we each need to determine and fulfill God's calling for us. Romans 11:29 states, "God's gifts and his call are irrevocable." Ephesians 2:10 states, "We are God's handiwork, created in Christ Jesus to do good works, which God prepared in advance for us to do."

And note that what David said to God in Psalm 139:13–16 applies to us as well.

For you created my inmost being; you knit me together in my mother's womb. I praise you because I am fearfully and wonderfully made; your works are wonderful, I know that full well. My frame was not hidden from you when I was made in the secret place, when I was woven together in the depths of the earth. Your eyes saw my unformed body; all the days ordained for me were written in your book before one of them came to be.

Hence God has a specific calling for you. So wise Christians consider the natural talents and spiritual gifts God has given them and then prayerfully discern his calling.

In summary, fulfill God's calling with your time, money, and talents so that when you get to heaven, you will hear the words you want to hear from the Lord: "Well done, good and faithful servant! You have been faithful with a few things; I will put you in charge of many things. Come and share your master's happiness!" (Matthew 25:23).

28. Christians as Bad Stewards

For those Christians who have not used money, material things, their time, or spiritual gifts for the kingdom of God, they will suffer loss by having very few rewards in heaven. Believers in Jesus Christ will be saved and will spend eternity in heaven. However, there is no second chance for anyone to come back to this fallen world and invest money, time, and talents for God's kingdom that will result in rewards in heaven.

Once we die, it's too late to go back and change our lives. So wise Christians invest their money, time, and talents in areas of eternal value. When we get to heaven, I suspect many Christians will wish they had avoided unnecessary expenses, spent less on themselves, and given more to God's work.

In summary, I encourage you to learn and apply God's word on finances and give generously to God's work with respect to money, time, and talents. After that, you can trust God to reward you generously in heaven!

29. What About Non-Christians?

Only Christians will appear before the judgment seat of Christ. Overall, it will be a good time as believers will receive rewards based upon their faithfulness to God.

As for the non-believers, they will appear before the great white throne of judgment as described in Revelation 20. I need to speak the truth in love to those people who have never accepted Jesus Christ as their Saviour and Lord, for their eternal benefit.

Hebrews 9:27 states, "People are destined to die once, and after that to face judgment." And 1 John 5:11–13 states, "God has given us eternal life, and this life is in his Son. Whoever has the Son has life; whoever does not have the Son of God does not have life."

In this verse, life refers to eternal life in heaven with God. Therefore, non-Christians will not be spending eternity in heaven because of their decision not to accept Christ as Saviour and Lord. I would encourage all non-believers to accept Christ as Saviour and Lord today.

In conclusion, I encourage all non-believers to acknowledge that you are sinners (Romans 3:23) and believe that Jesus Christ died for your sins. Accept Christ as Saviour and Lord today. Do not procrastinate—this decision is critical as it will impact where you spend eternity after you die.

30. The Great White Throne of Judgment

Revelation 20:11–15 describes the great white throne of judgment of non-believers. Note that the dead refers to those who are spiritually dead and have had no relationship with Christ. In other words, they never accepted Jesus Christ as Saviour and Lord while they were alive.

Then I saw a great white throne and him who was seated on it. The earth and the heavens fled from his presence, and there was no place for them. And I saw the
dead, great and small, standing before the throne, and
books were opened. Another book was opened, which is
the book of life. The dead were judged according to what
they had done as recorded in the books. The sea gave
up the dead that were in it, and death and Hades gave
up the dead that were in them, and each person was
judged according to what they had done. Then death and
Hades were thrown into the lake of fire. The lake of fire
is the second death. Anyone whose name was not found
written in the book of life was thrown into the lake of fire.

Please understand that if you decide not to accept Christ as
your Saviour and Lord, then you will spend eternity in the lake of
fire. I want you to avoid that, so I encourage you to accept Jesus
Christ as Saviour and Lord today.

31. The Difference Between the Judgment Seat of Christ and the Great White Throne

Although genuine Christians will be forgiven for their sins and
spend eternity in heaven, they will nevertheless appear before
God at the judgment seat of Christ (2 Corinthians 5:10) and
receive rewards or suffer loss due to lack of rewards according
to how they used the money, time, and talents God entrusted
to them while they were on earth (1 Corinthians 3:10–15; 1
Corinthians 4:2).

For those who have served Christ faithfully with their time,
talent, and money, appearing before the judgment seat of Christ
will be a time of great celebration. As for non-believers, they will
stand before God at the great white throne (Revelation 20:11–

15) and will not be forgiven for their sins and will spend eternity in the lake of fire.

The punishment for some non-believers will be worse than it is for others, depending upon what each person has done; their actions are recorded in God's books (Revelation 20:12). If you have never accepted Jesus Christ as Saviour and Lord, I encourage you to do so today. Don't wait; you never know when you will die.

32. Gospel Presentation

If you have never accepted Jesus Christ as your personal Saviour, I encourage you to seriously consider the following things.

God loves you and God wants a personal relationship with you. However, our sins have separated us from God. Romans 3:23 states, "For all have sinned and fall short of the glory of God."

Many people seek God the wrong way, such as believing good works, religions, philosophy, or morality can save them. However, none of our efforts can bridge this gap between God and humans because no human being is holy and perfect like God. God has provided the only solution through Jesus Christ. Romans 5:8 states, "God demonstrates his own love for us in this: While we were still sinners, Christ died for us."

In summary, Jesus Christ died on the cross for our sins. If you believe that and accept Christ as your Saviour and Lord, then you can have a personal relationship with Christ and spend eternity in heaven. I encourage you to make this decision today.

33. God Will Judge Appropriately

Scripture is clear that God will judge both good and evil. Romans 2:6 says, "God 'will repay each person according to what they have done.'" To those who by persistence in doing good seek glory, honour, and immortality, he will give eternal life.

But for those who are self-seeking and who reject the truth and follow evil, there will be wrath and anger. "There will be trouble and distress for every human being who does evil: first for the Jew, then for the Gentile; but glory, honor and peace for everyone who does good: first for the Jew, then for the Gentile" (Romans 2:9–10).

When Christians do good things with money, God will bless them both here on earth and in heaven for eternity. Some of the good things we can use money for are giving to Christian ministries who do evangelism, discipleship, or helping the poor. Jesus said that when you help the poor, "although they cannot repay you, you will be repaid at the resurrection of the righteous" (Luke 14:13–14).

In summary, use money for good things that the Lord would approve of.

34. There Will Be Crowns in Heaven for Faithful Believers

Here are some of the crowns that God will grant to faithful believers.

1. An incorruptible crown. In 1 Corinthians 9:24–25, Paul compared our life here on earth to a race. "Do you not know that in a race all the runners run, but only one gets the prize? Run in such a way as to get the prize. Everyone who competes in the games goes into strict training. They do it to get a crown that will not last, but we do it to get a crown that will last forever."

2. The crown of life. James 1:12 states, "Blessed is the one who perseveres under trial because, having stood

the test, that person will receive the crown of life that the Lord has promised to those who love him."

3. The crown of righteousness. Paul said, "I have fought the good fight, I have finished the race, I have kept the faith. Now there is in store for me the crown of right- eousness, which the Lord, the righteous Judge, will award to me on that day" (2 Timothy 4:7–8).

Have you kept the faith with respect to stewardship of the resources that God has given you?

35. Summary: Money Management Impacts Eternity

When we get to heaven and stand before Christ, here are some questions that God could ask.

What did you do with the money and material things I en- trusted to you (1 Corinthians 4:2)? Did you spend it unneces- sarily, perhaps on your own selfish desires, or did you invest my money in my work? As you did things for me, the Lord, were your motives pure or selfish (Proverbs 16:2)?

How did you use the time, natural talents, and spiritual gifts I gave to you? Did you waste them on things that are temporary in nature? Or did you focus on things of eternal value (Colos- sians 3:1–2), such as involvement in evangelism and discipling people?

Remember, if you do not manage money God's way, you may have few rewards in heaven. And once you've died, you cannot come back to this earth and do life all over again.

In summary, be sure to invest the money, time, and talents that God has entrusted to you for eternal purposes!

If you would like to learn more about how money manage- ment impacts eternity, watch the three half-hour videos on this topic available at www.coplandfinancialministries.org. We have numerous other resources there as well, most of which are free. You can also follow @biblefinance on Facebook, Instagram, and Twitter.

COPLAND FINANCIAL MINISTRIES RESOURCES

As of the time of writing this book, here is an overview of the resources available at www.coplandfinancialministries.org.

1. Financial Management God's Way: participant's copy and leader's guide. This resource is very suitable for small group studies; however, individuals and couples can also study it on their own, or they can join one of our Zoom small groups.
2. Financial Management God's Way: online interactive video. This is a great way to learn God's word on finances. Many small group leaders have found that using this video series makes it easy to lead a small group financial study. This online interactive series is available on an ongoing basis on our website.
3. Discerning God's Will in Managing Money: advanced workshop with eight half-hour videos.
4. Debt Reduction God's Way: DVD/CD workshop and online series.
5. God's Financial Wisdom for Business: CD and online series.
6. Debt Reduction God's Way for Business: CD and online series.
7. Biblically Based Estate Planning: CD and online series.
8. Tom's Top Financial Moments: single CD with 70 financial moments.
9. Copland Budgeting System: free downloadable Excel-based form.

10. Financial Moments Podcast: online video and audio.
11. Numerous half-hour videos on many different financial topics.
12. Numerous written articles and many other resources.
13. Financial Moment email list. Be sure to register for this on our website so you can receive a financial moment each week and be advised of upcoming workshops in person and on Zoom.
14. Biblically based financial coaching, which is provided on a ministry basis at no charge. Go to the website and send us an email.

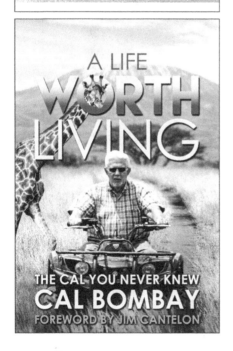

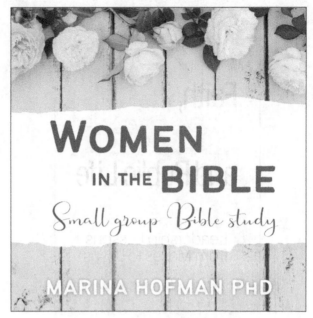